Deadly Women
Volume Eight

20 Shocking
True Murder Cases

Robert Keller

**Please Leave Your Review of This Book At
http://bit.ly/kellerbooks**

ISBN-9798620954933

© 2020 by Robert Keller

robertkellerauthor.com

Table of Contents

Beth Carpenter

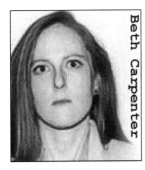

It started on a pleasant Connecticut evening in March 1994, when police received reports of a body lying at the side of a remote stretch of road just off I-95. Officers of the East Lyme PD responded, expecting to find the victim of a traffic accident. What they found instead was a murder scene. Five bullets had been pumped into the dead man, a man they all knew well. He was 28-year-old Anson Clinton III, known to his friends as Buzz.

The officers were not exactly surprised by the identity of the victim. Buzz Clinton was a man with a lot of enemies. He was a somewhat rowdy local, a drug user and reputedly a small-time dealer, someone who scrounged a living doing odd jobs, when he could be bothered to work at all. Most recently, he'd been performing at local clubs as a male stripper, but Buzz's dancing days were over now. Five bullets from a .38 had seen to that. Who had fired those fatal shots? Some rival drug dealer was what the police initially surmised. They were wrong.

Two months passed, with the police making very little headway in tracking down Buzz Clinton's killer. Then, in May of 1994, there was a surprise break in the case. A woman named Cathy White called investigators and said that she had information to share. Her boyfriend, Joseph Fremut, was involved in the murder of Buzz Clinton, along with a man named Mark Depres. Both men were well known to the East Lyme police. Both had extensive rap sheets while Depres was an occasional informant. It was on this pretext that officers lured him to a meeting. Depres, who thought that he was going to be asked about some or other drug deal, suddenly found himself being quizzed about a murder.

Depres, however, had danced this dance before. He was not about to be strong- armed by a couple of small town cops. He refused to answer questions and insisted on contacting his lawyer. When the cops allowed him to do so, he made several attempts to contact a local attorney, Haiman Clein. This appeared a strange choice to the officers. Clein was well-known locally as a high-powered real estate lawyer. He didn't handle criminal work. Besides, he was well out of Depres's price range. On this day, he was also not taking calls. Unable to reach him, Depres eventually agreed to talk to Detective Chet Harris, the officer who occasionally used him as a C.I. (confidential informant). During the course of that conversation, Depres admitted that he did have information about Buzz Clinton's death and that he "may have been involved."

But the identification of Depres as a murder suspect was just the start of what was to become an incredibly complex case. Depres claimed that he'd gunned down Clinton on the orders of Haiman Clein, the lawyer he'd been trying to reach. But what interest did Clein, a multi-millionaire fixer for the rich and famous, have in a nobody like Buzz Clinton? The answer to that question would lead to an even less likely suspect, a brilliant young lawyer named Beth Ann Carpenter, who happened to be Buzz Clinton's sister-in-law.

Beth Carpenter was born on November 2, 1963, and grew up just a few miles from the Long Island Sound, near Old Saybrook. The area is picturesque and affluent, and Beth was raised in a happy, tight-knit family unit. She excelled at school, scoring straight A's, and was eventually accepted at George Washington University. Her plan was to attend medical school after college, but a last minute change of heart saw her decide to study law instead. That took her to Catholic University and later to an internship at the SEC. After passing the bar exams in Connecticut, New York, and Washington D.C., she was ready to take on the world.

The early nineties, however, was not a great time for a young lawyer to be in the job market. Beth drew more than a few blanks until the day that she walked into the New London law offices of Haiman Clein. He hired her on the spot. So began a working relationship that would soon develop into something more. Clein was 52 years old at the time and on his fourth marriage; Beth was 29 and still somewhat naive. He was overweight, balding, and heavy-jowled; she was lithe, with striking blue eyes and a mane of auburn hair. It is difficult to see what the attraction was. Nonetheless, a torrid sexual relationship developed. Soon the couple were sharing pillow talk. One of Beth's preoccupations at that time was the welfare of her three-year-old niece, Rebecca, the daughter of her sister, Kim.

Kim and Beth Carpenter could not have been more different. Whereas Beth was academically gifted and the shining light of the Carpenter clan, Kim had grown up with a learning disability and had flunked out of school without graduating. She'd then compounded her childhood problems by making bad choices as an adult. Her first husband (Rebecca's father) was a jailbird who had been sent down for a long stretch even before the birth of his daughter. Kim had divorced him while he was serving his time. She'd then hooked up with Buzz Clinton, who she'd met on a night out, at a club where he was dancing. Kim's family had been less than impressed with Buzz, their distaste amplified when he and Kim disappeared for six weeks after their first meeting, leaving little Rebecca in the care of her grandparents. During that time, Kim had not even bothered to visit her baby daughter, not even once. Kim did eventually show up at the house, but only to tell her parents that she and Buzz were getting married.

For Kim and Beth's mother, Cynthia, it was the last straw. Afraid of what would happen to Rebecca in the dubious care of Kim and Buzz, she decided to petition for custody. With a lawyer in the family, she had every confidence in winning, more so when Kim arrived at the court without an attorney. Her new husband, Buzz, would argue the case on her behalf. Buzz, as it turns out, was quite eloquent. Despite having no legal training at all, he won. Then he and Kim compounded the family feud by announcing that they were moving to Arizona, taking Rebecca with them. It was at this point that Beth turned to her boss and lover, Haiman Clein, for help. Clein said that he knew someone who could take care of the problem, a guy who sometimes supplied him with cocaine – Mark Depres.

Whether or not Beth Ann directly asked Clein to arrange a hit on Buzz Clinton, we will never know for certain. Clein says that she did, and since the jury accepted his version of events, we must assume that to be the case. In any event, Depres was offered $8,500 to murder Buzz and accepted $2,000 as a down payment. The opportunity to carry out the hit arose in March 1994 when Buzz placed an ad in the local newspaper offering his tow truck for sale. The first call that he got was from Mark Depres, saying that he was interested in viewing the vehicle. The two of them agreed to meet in the parking lot of a diner along I-95 on March 10. From there, Depres could follow Buzz to where he was garaging the vehicle.

Originally, the plan had been for Joseph Fremut to accompany Depres on the hit. But Fremut was feeling unwell that day, and so Depres roped in his own 15-year-old son to ride along. After meeting at the diner, the three of them set off, with Depres following Buzz's bronze-colored Camaro. They had just left the I-95 when Depres flashed his lights, indicating that Buzz should pull over. Buzz complied. He was just getting out of his vehicle when Depres approached, pulled a .38 and gunned him down. Depres and his son then sped away from the scene, driving over Buzz's body as they did.

That was how the murder went down, according to Depres. It had been a hit arranged by Haiman Clein on behalf of his girlfriend. But proving it would be a different matter. The word of a habitual criminal does not usually carry much weight in a court of law. The police did not even have the murder weapon, which Depres had destroyed directly after the murder. Desperate for something, anything, that would back up Depres's statement, detectives then began delving into Clein's affairs and uncovered that he was involved in far more than the murder-for-hire plot. He had been defrauding clients, dipping into trust accounts, and dealing dope. He also had a voracious sexual appetite. Beth Carpenter was just one of his many conquests.

But Beth had moved on now, quitting her job in January 1995 and relocating to London, England, where a friend had found her a position with a reputable law firm. She still remained in touch with Clein, though. The two spoke regularly on the phone. That was probably how she learned that Mark Depres had been arrested and charged with Buzz's murder. A short while later, she quit her high-paying London job and moved to Dublin, Ireland, where she found work as a waitress. The reason for this sudden move seems obvious in retrospect. Ireland does not extradite suspects to a jurisdiction where they might face execution. In Connecticut, a conviction in a murder-for-hire case usually results in that sanction.

While Mark Depres languished in a Connecticut jail and Beth Carpenter was serving up pints of Guinness in a Dublin pub, the third member of the deadly trio had gone into hiding. When officers arrived with an arrest warrant on December 15, 1995, they found Haiman Clein missing and his clients' accounts severely depleted.

Clein would remain on the run for two months. During that time, he was in constant contact with Beth Carpenter, calling her cell from various payphones. He could not have known that the U.S. authorities had been in touch with Beth, asking for her assistance in apprehending him. Perhaps thinking that it would count in her favor should she ever go on trial, Beth agreed.

In February 2006, Clein arrived at a payphone in Sunset, California, to wait for a prearranged call from Beth. They had just begun their conversation when Federal agents moved in and snapped the cuffs on Clein. His last words to his former lover were, "You set me up."

With two of the murder suspects now in custody, the authorities threw their full weight behind bringing Beth Carpenter back to the U.S. to face the music. That would require some deft maneuvering. The Irish authorities were initially reluctant to extradite Carpenter, although they did agree to arrest her and hold her in custody to prevent her from fleeing the country. She would remain in an Irish prison for 19 months before a deal was struck. Ireland would send her back. In exchange, the State of Connecticut agreed not to pursue the death penalty in her case.

By the time Beth Ann Carpenter arrived back in the United States in November 1997, her co-accused had already pled guilty to the charges against them and accepted the terms that were on offer – 45 years for each of them. Mark Despres had initially agreed that he would testify at the Carpenter trial but later withdrew his offer and refused to co-operate. The same could not be said for Haiman Clein. He was thirsty for revenge over Beth's betrayal and ready to tell all. In fact, one of the prosecutors called him "the most cooperative witness that I have ever worked with."

And so to the 2002 capital murder trial of Beth Ann Carpenter. The death penalty was, of course, off the table, but the stakes could not have been higher. Here was a beautiful and accomplished young woman facing a lifetime behind bars if found guilty. It all came down to two competing narratives. On the one hand, there was Beth's story. In it, she admitted that she had complained frequently to Clein about the custody situation with her niece Rebecca. However, she denied that she had ever asked Clein to have Buzz Clinton killed. She claimed that the murder was all Clein's doing. He had arranged it in order to impress her. The first she'd heard about Buzz's death was when she saw it on the news.

Clein, however, told a different story. According to him, Beth had pestered him constantly to find someone to get rid of Buzz. Clein had been reluctant at first, but had eventually agreed after Beth told him that Buzz was sexually and physically abusing the toddler. According to her, the family had noticed several circular marks on the little girl's skin that turned out to be cigarette burns. It was only to spare the child further harm that he had agreed to find a hitman.

Haiman Clein had been impressive on the stand; Beth Carpenter less so. Whereas he spoke clearly and authoritatively with a good recall of facts and dates, she stuttered and stammered, sometimes seemed confused, and often answered with "I don't remember." Perhaps that was what swung it for the jury. After deliberating for four days, they returned with a verdict of guilty of capital murder and guilty of conspiracy to commit murder.

Beth Carpenter was sentenced to life in prison without possibility of parole. She is currently held at Janet S. York Correctional Institution in Niantic, Connecticut. For his part in helping obtain a conviction against his former lover, Haiman Clein was given a ten-year reduction of his sentence. Ironically, Kim Carpenter subsequently signed over custody of her daughter, Rebecca, to her parents. The murder of Buzz Clinton might all have been for nothing.

Valerie Pape

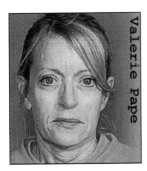

The car was a top-of-the-range Jaguar, its occupant, a petite blonde, dressed in an animal-print jumpsuit and stiletto heels. The question was: what was she doing here, behind a Mesa, Arizona, strip mall in the dead of night?

To the deliveryman who had watched the car pull up and its glamorous driver get out, the mystery deepened even further when the woman walked around to the trunk and flipped it open. Then she appeared to be struggling to remove some heavy object, then she had it in her grasp and was staggering with it towards a dumpster. Finally, after some effort, she was able to heft this object over the rim and into the steel container. That done, the woman walked quickly back to her car and sped off. The deliveryman, seated in his van and hidden in the shadows, wrote down her license plate number before she disappeared into the night.

Now the deliveryman had a decision to make. Should he call the police to report this odd encounter, or should he walk over to the dumpster to see what it was that the blonde had left there? Every instinct in his body told him that this was a matter for the police. An object dumped late at night, in a concealed location, was likely to involve some kind of illegality. Yet the driver was curious, and so he decided to take a peek. Getting out of his van, he walked across the tarmac and peered over the rim into the dumpster. There, in the dim glow of an overhead light, sat the package, a chunky piece of something wrapped in black garbage bags. It gave off a slightly funky smell that set alarm bells jangling. The deliveryman thought again of calling the police. But, he'd come this far, and now he was determined to get to the bottom of the mystery. He reached in, started tearing at the plastic wrapping, and soon wished that he hadn't. The package contained a human torso.

With a license plate number in hand, tracking the mystery blonde was a simple matter. She was 47-year-old Valerie Pape, a French national who ran a ritzy beauty salon in Scottsdale, Arizona, catering to the city's wealthiest women. Pape was married to a prominent businessman named Ira Pomerantz, thirteen years her senior. The couple lived in a luxury villa in McCormick Ranch, an exclusive Scottsdale neighborhood. Local police officers were well acquainted with the pair. They had been called out to domestic disturbances at their residence on numerous occasions.

Valerie was at home when detectives called on her. She willingly let them in and even allowed them to carry out a search. But her cooperation would land her in trouble. The officers quickly found evidence of foul play, including blood spatters in the garage, a recent receipt for a reciprocating saw, a spent bullet in the kitchen, and a 9mm pistol hidden behind the back seat of her Jaguar. Pape also could not account for her husband's whereabouts, saying that they had recently been living apart due to marital differences. With the evidence that the police already had against her, that was never going to fly. Valerie was led away from her house in handcuffs that day.

Valerie Pape was not your typical psycho killer. Those who knew her described the petite beautician as friendly, charming, elegant, sophisticated. It was difficult to imagine her killing someone, let alone hacking a body apart with an electric saw. Yet the case against Pape was overwhelming. She was now looking at a first-degree murder conviction, in a state that still had the death penalty on its statute books. It was no surprise when her lawyer approached prosecutors for a plea deal. Pape would offer a full confession to second-degree murder. Since there was no specific evidence of premeditation, the D.A. agreed.

The explanation that Valerie Pape offered for her husband's death was simple. She was a battered wife who had finally fought back. Pape had immigrated to the United States in the early 90s. She had settled in Scottsdale and had opened her salon which soon became a favorite with the city's society ladies. She was doing quite well for herself but still longed for companionship. One night, while dining out alone, a man had approached and introduced himself as Ira Pomerantz, the owner of the restaurant. He and Valerie had enjoyed a glass of champagne together, and Ira had asked if she would have dinner with him sometime. He was handsome, articulate, and quite obviously wealthy, and so she'd said yes. That first date had gone well and, soon after, they were an item. Within a year, Ira had asked her to marry him, and Valerie had accepted.

Being the wife of a wealthy entrepreneur had obvious benefits. Valerie lived in a luxury home, drove the latest model Jag, enjoyed shopping trips and exotic holidays. But life with Ira was not all wine and roses, as Valerie was soon to discover. He had a temper and could be verbally and physically abusive. The couple fought often, and their fights grew more and more frequent as the decade wore on and Ira started running into financial problems in his businesses. During this time, Valerie's friends and customers often noticed bruises on her face, despite her efforts to cover up the injuries with makeup.

The spousal disputes during this turbulent period were usually about money. Ira demanded that Valerie cut down on her spending, but Valerie seldom paid heed to these warnings and continued running up credit card bills. But then, in the late 90s, there was another bone of contention. Terrified of her husband's violent outbursts, Valerie invited a friend from her homeland, Michael Sauvage, to live with them. The arrangement was supposed to last for a few weeks, but Sauvage ended up staying for over a year. And rather than calming the tensions between the couple, his presence escalated their problems. On several occasions, Ira ordered his wife's guest from the house only for Valerie to countermand him and tell Sauvage to stay. Then Ira moved out, although he soon returned.

Sauvage's presence also gave Ira a new accusation to level at his wife. He accused her of sleeping with their houseguest, sparking a whole new round of confrontations. On one occasion, Valerie dialed 911 and told the dispatcher that her husband was throwing kitchen knives at her. That incident resulted in a restraining order being issued and Ira being forced to move out of his own home. During his absence, Valerie bought herself a gun and started taking shooting lessons. According to her instructor, she went from complete novice to crack shot in record time.

And so to the night of January 23, 2004, the night that the disagreements between Valerie and Ira turned deadly. According to Valerie, she returned home that night to find Ira inebriated and belligerent. He demanded to know why she was late and refused to accept her explanation that she had been at the salon. At one point, he slapped her across the face. Then he turned his back on her and walked towards the bar to pour himself another drink. It was then that Valerie took her gun out of her handbag, walked up behind Ira and pumped four rounds into his back. It was self-preservation rather than self-defense. She had feared that she was going to be beaten again and had struck first, before Ira could attack her.

But now, Valerie had a problem, a dead body in the living room and a smoking gun in her hand. The sensible thing to do would have been to call the police, to explain that she had acted in self-defense, to hope that the courts accepted her story and were sensitive to her plight as a battered wife. But Valerie was terrified that she would not be believed, that she'd end up with a life sentence or maybe even on death row. And so she came to a desperate decision; she decided to make her husband disappear.

Disposing of a human body is no easy matter, and it is certainly not for the faint of heart. First, Valerie dragged the corpse into the garage and laid it out on some plastic sheeting. After leaving it there overnight, she went the next day to a hardware store and purchased a reciprocating saw and several spare blades. This she used to saw off her husband's head, his arms and legs, taking four days over the tasks, working in short bursts, as long as her gag reflex held. The body parts were then wrapped in plastic and left in the garage while Valerie decided what to do with them. The head and appendages would be disposed of first, in locations that Valerie Pape has always refused to reveal. However, it was the disposal of the torso that would lead to her downfall.

Valerie had initially intended to dump the remains in the desert, but she'd become increasingly unnerved over the mutilated corpse sitting in her garage. Eventually, she'd panicked, loaded the torso into her Jaguar and driven with it to Mesa, where she was spotted by the deliveryman. It is highly unlikely that she'd have gotten away with the murder anyway. Ira would undoubtedly have been missed, and Valerie had done a poor job of cleaning up the crime scene. Her ill-advised dumping of the torso merely accelerated her arrest.

Valerie Pape entered a guilty plea at her 2002 trial and was sentenced to sixteen years behind bars. In 2016, she was deported and transferred to a French prison. She was released two years later, in 2018.

Penny Bjorkland

On a warm, breezy Sunday afternoon in February 1959, 30-year-old gardener August Norry loaded up his truck with lawn cuttings and drove into the San Bruno Mountains, just south of San Francisco, where he planned on dumping the waste. Norry, a military veteran who had been wounded during the Korean conflict, was married 18 months and had a baby on the way. He was employed as a full-time landscaper at the Lake Merced Country Club but had recently taken on extra work to ensure that his child would lack for nothing when it arrived. That was how he came to be working on a Sunday.

But this day would be different to any other. When August failed to return from his trip into the mountains, his wife Darlene became concerned. Later that night, she reported him missing. At around the time that that report was being filed, the police in San Leandro were dealing with another matter. A truck had been found abandoned on a lover's lane near Christmas Tree Hill. Blood inside the vehicle suggested something amiss. The mystery would be resolved early the following morning when a report came in about a bullet-riddled body, found beside a road in the foothills. It was August Norry.

The extreme overkill employed in the crime suggested to the police that this was personal. Norry had been shot eighteen times, which meant that the killer had reloaded and continued firing, even after he was dead. The angle of the bullet wounds showed that the first shots had been fired while Norry was in the driver's seat. The killer had then exited the vehicle, walked around it, opened the driver's door, and continued shooting. Norry was then dragged out and dumped face down on the ground. Yet even now, the killer's bloodlust was not sated. Six more bullets were fired into the corpse. August Norry had been shot three times in the head, three times in the neck, three times in the chest, twice in the stomach, and several times in his arms and legs. It was as though his killer had been intent on completely obliterating him.

But who had committed this savage crime? The police had a theory. August Norry was a handsome and charismatic man. Before joining the army, he had been a minor league baseball player. He had also worked as a dance instructor at Arthur Murray. Investigators believed that he'd been having an affair and had probably been killed by his lover or by a jealous husband or boyfriend. Darlene Norry assured them that they were wrong. Augie was not that kind of man. But the police would soon have validation for their theory. A young boy came forward to report that he had seen a truck driving erratically and at high speed on the afternoon that Norry was killed. According to the witness, the person behind the wheel had been a young blonde. All efforts now focused on tracking down this mystery woman.

Presented with a description of this suspect, Darlene Norry remained adamant that neither she nor her husband knew such a person. Unconvinced, Daly City and San Mateo County Police carried out a search of the Norry home. They were hoping to find a journal or perhaps some correspondence that might have passed between Norry and their blonde suspect. They came away empty handed.

Questioning Norry's co-workers also proved frustrating. Although some of them thought that he might have been seeing someone on the side, most described him as a "stand-up guy" with no enemies. They were mystified as to why anyone might have wanted him dead. Detectives heard the same story from the victim's family and in-laws. August Norry was an average, friendly, hard-working family man who was looking forward to the birth of his first child. He had few close friends and didn't socialize much. He was hardly a high-risk victim.

And yet someone had taken it into their mind that Norry had to die and had killed him in a way that indicated extreme anger. Something wasn't adding up here. In an attempt to unravel the mystery, San Mateo detectives focused on the only real clue they had, the bullets that had killed August Norry. Fortunately, these were unusual. They were .38 caliber rounds of the kind used mostly by enthusiasts who reload their own ammunition using a bullet mold.

Detectives Milt Minehan and Willam Ridenour were given the arduous task of tracking down the manufacturer of the mold. This was particularly difficult since the maker might be based anywhere in the United States. Eventually, after nearly three months, the detectives zeroed in on a small company in New Jersey who confirmed that the mold was theirs. Ten thousand had been sold nationally, but for now Minehan and Ridenour were only interested in sales to the Bay Area. Their inquiries would eventually lead them to 23-year-old car mechanic and gun nut Lawrence Schultze.

Schultze was initially cagey when the detectives called, insisting that he only made bullets for his own target practice. But after samples of his gun lead were found to match the slugs pulled from August Norry, Schultze eventually admitted that he had sold a box of 50 bullets to his girlfriend's best friend, 18-year-old Rosemarie "Penny" Bjorkland. He also said that Bjorkland often practiced her shooting in the San Bruno Mountains, close to the location where Norry's body had been found. "Is she a blonde?" Det. Minehan asked. To this, a slightly bemused Schultze replied, "Yes."

The next day, April 15, 1959, officers arrived at the Bjorkland residence, in a working class neighborhood of Daly City, just south of the San Francisco city limits. Penny Bjorkland, by now the prime suspect in a brutal murder, turned out to be the picture of normality, a pretty, freckled-faced 18-year-old who wore her strawberry-blonde hair in a ponytail. She seemed unfazed by having the police in her home and readily gave them permission to search her room, where they found a shoebox full of newspaper clippings about the Norry murder. To the astonishment of her parents and three brothers, Penny was then placed under arrest and led from the house in cuffs.

Under interrogation at the San Mateo Sheriff's Department, Penny Bjorkland initially refused to answer questions. However, police persistence eventually wore her down. At 5:40 in the morning, she eventually confessed. A few hours later, she was taken back to the scene of her crime, where she reenacted the shooting for detectives and assembled members of the press corps. The newspapers would later report that she giggled as she described the murder. They attributed this to malice, ignoring the fact that the 18-year-old might simply have been nervous in recreating her crime for an audience.

What the police still didn't know was why she'd done it. Had she known August Norry? Had she been involved in a relationship with him? The answer to both of those questions was an emphatic "no." Norry was a complete stranger who Penny Bjorkland had shot on the spur of the moment. In doing so, she had fulfilled a long-held ambition. According to Penny, she had been fantasizing about killing someone for years.

Describing her actions on the day of the murder, Bjorkland said that she had gone into the hills that Sunday to do some target practice, as was her habit. She had been walking along the road with her pistol concealed in her waistband when Norry had stopped to offer her a ride. She'd accepted, but they had covered only a short distance when she drew her weapon and fired out of the window of the moving vehicle. Norry had then brought the truck to a stop and berated her for being so reckless. They had then talked for a few minutes. All the while, Bjorkland had been itching to point the gun at him and pull the trigger. Eventually, the compulsion had gotten the best of her.

Norry had been caught entirely by surprise. He'd not even had time to get out a cry before the first shot rang out. Most likely, that bullet, fired into his chest, had killed him. Bjorkland, however, had continued pulling the trigger, firing until the hammer fell on an empty chamber. She'd then gotten out of the vehicle and walked around to the driver's side. There she had reloaded, opened the door and pumped six more bullets into Norry's corpse. Then she'd pushed him into the passenger seat and driven the vehicle to an isolated road where she pulled the lifeless body out into the open. There she'd again reloaded the .38 and pumped six more slugs into the very dead body of August Norry. She'd then driven the truck away, ditching it some distance off and walking the rest of the way home. She had arrived just in time for Sunday dinner, which she had enjoyed with her family. The following day, she had dumped the gun and the unused bullets into a storm drain near her home.

"After it was done, I felt much better mentally," Bjorkland explained to detectives. "Like a great burden had been lifted off of me. I have no bad memories about it. I always wanted to see if I could do something like this and not have it bother me."

It was a murder unlike any seen in the United States since perhaps the Leopold and Loeb case 35 years earlier. Here was a polite, attractive, apparently normal teenager, gunning down a complete stranger for no other reason than to see how it felt. Delving into Bjorkland's background, investigators did find some indicators that all was not as it should be with the teen. Penny had been a loner at school and had often carried a large hunting knife in her book bag, sometimes showing it off to horrified classmates. The knife had later been replaced by the .38, which she'd stolen from her boyfriend's parents' home. Still, no one would have expected her to use that gun in a murder. How did one make sense of this inexplicable crime? Was it even possible to explain?

Perhaps not. Bjorkland, in any case, declined to have her mental state examined. She refused to speak to a psychiatrist and even sent away the family priest when he tried to visit. She was guilty, she said, and was willing to accept the consequences. Neither her attorney nor her parents could persuade her to put forward an insanity defense.

On July 20, 1959, Penny Bjorkland pled guilty to the charge of second-degree murder and was sentenced to life in prison with parole eligibility in seven years. She would serve that minimum term at the California State Prison for Women at Corona before being released in the mid-Sixties and promptly dropping out of sight. There is no record of her whereabouts or fate after she was set free.

Darlene Norry gave birth to a daughter, Cynthia, on September 17, 1959. The little girl would grow up never knowing her father, a good man who stopped to offer help to a stranger on a sunny afternoon and ended up shot to death on a whim.

Zatoon Bibi

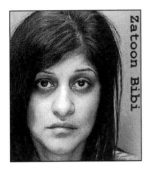

The year was 2008, and in the city of Birmingham, England, Tanveer Iqbal was living the good life. Tall, handsome, and outgoing, Tanveer had two overriding interests – music and women. His chosen career, as the owner of a popular record shop, gave him access to both, the latter in the form of attractive female customers. One of them, a regular, was named Zatoon Bibi.

Zatoon was, like Tanveer, a far from traditional Muslim. She preferred western clothes and culture and seldom wore a hijab. Despite these modernist leanings, though, Zatoon had not escaped all of the influences of her society. She was in an arranged marriage to a man thirteen years her senior. At 31, she was the mother of four children.

And so, Zatoon rebuffed Tanveer's initial efforts to flirt with her, telling him that she was a wife and mom. His response was that he was married, too, but that seemed to hold little sway. Not that Tanveer was discouraged; he kept at it and gradually wore Zatoon down.

Eventually, he persuaded her to join him for an assignation in a hotel room. That was the first time that Zatoon had had sex with anyone other than her husband, and the encounter left her deeply ashamed. She told Tanveer that they could never be together again. Reluctantly, he accepted her decision, chalking their encounter off as a one-night stand.

But that one-night stand would have significant, life-changing consequences. Shortly after they slept together, Zatoon discovered that she was pregnant. In 2009, she gave birth to a baby girl which her husband, Gul Nawaz, accepted as his own. Zatoon knew different, though. She revealed to Tanveer that the child was his and started visiting him at the music store so that he could get to know his daughter. Tanveer, who had no children with his wife at that time, doted on the little girl. And perhaps it was this devotion that won Zatoon over because she and Tanveer started sleeping together again.

Zatoon's double life, however, was soon to be exposed. One day, her husband was going through her things when he discovered the results of a DNA test, proving that he was not the baby's father. Understandably livid, he confronted Zatoon and forced her into a tearful confession. Thereafter, he declared a talaq, effectively divorcing his wife by repudiating the marriage. Zatoon was out on the streets. Fortunately, she had, in Tanveer, a devoted lover and father who supported both her and the baby.

Tanveer's wife, Nasreen, appears to have known about his relationship with Zatoon and to have accepted it. Indeed, the women became friends and would regularly text each other back and forth, keeping up their communication even after Tanveer forbade them from doing so.

But in Zatoon's case, at least, the friendship was a scam. At the same time that she was merrily exchanging texts with Nasreen, she was working on Tanveer, trying to persuade him to leave his wife. She had a second child by Tanveer now, and she wanted him all to herself. The fact that Tanveer and Nasreen also had two kids together seemed not to concern her.

By January 2016, Zatoon was getting desperate. All of her begging, her cajoling, her scheming, was getting her nowhere. Tanveer was adamant that he would not leave Nasreen and told her that she'd have to learn to live with it. Angry at this refusal, Zatoon resorted to desperate measures. She sent Nasreen a text containing a video of her and Tanveer engaged in a sex act. Her plan was to drive a wedge between the couple, but it backfired badly.

When Nasreen showed Tanveer the video, he was furious. He immediately got on the phone to Zatoon and told her that it was over between them. He would continue to support his children, but he wanted nothing more to do with her. No amount of begging and apologizing on Zatoon's part could get him to change his mind.

But Tanveer had badly miscalculated in his obstinate attitude towards his lover. They say that hell hath no fury like a woman scorned, and this scorned woman was furious indeed. She started plotting her revenge, roping in an unlikely ally, her ex-husband, Gul Nawaz. Humiliated by his wife's affair, Nawaz was more than willing to help.

January 31, 2016, was Tanveer Iqbal's 33rd birthday, with a party planned for him that night. Zatoon, of course, was not invited, but she felt that she had at least some claim on her former lover's time that day. Calling him at work, she asked him to stop by her house that evening on his way home. When Tanveer demurred, she said that his children wanted to wish him happy birthday and had baked a cake for him. He wouldn't want to disappoint them, would he? A devoted father, Tanveer was never going to refuse. He arrived just after six and walked straight into a trap.

Tanveer's kids weren't home when he arrived, but Zatoon Bibi and Gul Nawaz were, along with their 15-year-old son, Kasheen. Between the three of them, they beat Tanveer, wrestled him to the ground, looped a rope around his neck and strangled him to death on the living room floor. Thereafter, they forced his body into a cardboard box which they secured with duct tape. This macabre package was loaded into the trunk of Tanveer's Renault Clio which was driven to a busy road near the Edgbaston cricket ground and abandoned there. Tanveer Iqbal had dared to forsake a desperate and devious woman and had paid for it with his life.

Tanveer's disappearance was noticed almost immediately. When he failed to arrive for his birthday party, friends and family started calling around to all the places where he might have been. Unable to locate him, they went to the police and filed a missing person report. Some of Tanveer's friends then started their own search. The following morning, one of them found his vehicle abandoned at the roadside. The police were then called and soon made a macabre discovery in the trunk. Tanveer had been badly beaten, suffering multiple cuts and contusions. But it was a length of rope that had ended his life, a rope that was still in place, cutting into the flesh of his throat.

The murder of Tanveer Iqbal was not a well-planned crime.
Birmingham is one of the most heavily surveilled cities in the UK,
with CCTV cameras everywhere. It did not take the police long to pick
up Tanveer's Renault on surveillance footage. Zooming in revealed the
person behind the wheel. It was Zatoon Bibi.

Zatoon was soon in custody and quickly gave up her former husband,
Gul Nawaz, saying that it was he alone who had killed Tanveer. She
claimed that she was innocent and that she had only agreed to drive the
car because Nawaz had threatened her. She then sought to build on this
falsehood. When her son, Kasheen, came to visit, she briefed him on
what to say to the police, implicating Nawaz and exonerating the two
of them.

Unfortunately for Zatoon, all prison calls are recorded and her attempt
at conspiracy was caught on tape. Not only had she now confirmed her
involvement in the murder, she had also implicated her son. Kasheen
was placed under arrest soon after. Further evidence of his
involvement was uncovered when police found a security tape from a
Poundland store. It showed Gul Nawaz and his teenaged son shopping
for items that would later be used in the murder – rope, rubber gloves,
and a roll of silver duct tape.

Zatoon Bibi and her co-accused went on trial at the Birmingham
Crown Court in July 2017, with Zatoon pleading not guilty and
sticking to her story that she was an innocent bystander. The evidence,
however, said different. Aside from the CCTV footage and the
recording of the telephone conversation, there were several text
messages that she had sent to the victim on the day he died. These had

the clear intention of luring him to her house. In one of them, sent just hours before the murder, she'd typed: "Hope you like it" (the cake).

In the end, the outcome of the trial was never in doubt. All three defendants were found guilty and sentenced to life in prison. Kasheen Nawaz must serve six years before he can apply for parole. His parents were given much harsher terms. Gul Nawaz will remain behind bars for at least 25 years; Zatoon Bibi, the mastermind behind the murder plot, must serve a minimum of 27 years.

Sarah Mitchell

They say that blood is thicker than water and that families stick together no matter what. But like most truisms, this one is easy to vocalize and often difficult to live by. Take the case of Stevie Allman and Sarah Mitchell, for example. Stevie and Sarah were sisters, but beside that, they had very little in common. Stevie (at 52, the older of the siblings) was a hard-working and law-abiding citizen. She was much loved in her East Oakland, California, neighborhood for her tough stance on drugs. Stevie was a constant thorn in the side of local dealers. Often, she'd carry out surveillance on them, taking pictures of their illicit activities and passing them on to the police.

Stevie's sister, Sarah, was the polar opposite, a hard-partying, dope-smoking former prostitute who had worked barely a day in her life. She sustained herself by sponging off relatives, usually wearing out her welcome quite quickly and then moving on to the next one. In early 1997, it was Stevie's turn. Sarah showed up on her doorstep, looking for a place to stay, and Stevie could hardly say no. They were blood, after all.

But Stevie would soon come to regret her generosity. Sarah was a far from considerate houseguest. She contributed nothing to the household, not a dime, not even an occasional offer to help with the chores. She took plenty, though. Often she'd bring friends around for wild, impromptu parties that would continue late into the night. If Sarah asked her to turn the music down or to send her friends home, she'd refuse; she even bring marijuana into the house in defiance of her sister's strict anti-drug stance.

Stevie Allman might have put up with all of that, but what she wasn't about to tolerate was Sarah stealing from her. It started shortly after Sarah moved in, when Stevie began to notice that small amounts of cash were going missing from her purse. Then she started to see transactions on her credit cards that she didn't recognize. Finally, in late June 1997, there was a call from her bank. Sarah had walked into the branch and tried to cash one of Stevie's checks while posing as her sister. She had even presented ID. Unfortunately for her, the teller that she chose knew Stevie and thus blocked the transaction. The bank wanted to know if Stevie wanted to press charges. She declined, saying that it was a misunderstanding that she and her sister would resolve themselves.

And resolve it they did. When Stevie confronted her sister that night, Sarah was belligerent, going on the offensive. She accused Stevie of looking down on her just because she had fallen on hard times. Stevie assured her that this was not the case. She loved her sister and wanted to help. However, it was time for Sarah, a middle-aged woman, to grow up and take responsibility for her own life. Stevie would no longer tolerate the all-night parties, the use of drugs in her house. She would most certainly not abide Sarah stealing from her. In fact, she had decided that it would be better if Sarah left. She wanted her out within the next 24 hours.

Sarah Mitchell went to bed fuming that night, a thousand angry thoughts competing for attention in her brain. Living with Stevie had been Easy Street to her, a place to crash, regular meals, a steady stream of pilfered cash. Now all of that was being snatched away, casting her out into an uncertain future. It didn't seem to occur to her that she had brought this on herself, that her sister had been incredibly generous to her, and that she had abused that generosity. To her mind, she had been unfairly treated. That got her angry. It got her thinking. It dredged up a truly horrific idea from the depths of her dark soul.

While Stevie Allman lay sleeping that night, her sister Sarah went down to the basement and fetched a crowbar. She then returned with it to Stevie's room, standing over her sleeping form for just a moment before raising the metal bar over her head and bringing it down. Stevie was immediately knocked unconscious, which was probably a good thing because blow after blow rained down on her, caving in her skull and splattering the bedcovers, the walls, the ceiling, with blood and brain matter. By the time Sarah broke off the attack, her sister had been beaten to a pulp.

But now Sarah had a new problem. Stevie was a large, heavyset woman. Moving her body was going to be difficult. Sarah had not thought this through. In fact, she hadn't considered disposal of the corpse at all. Again, the basement provided the solution. There was a handheld band saw down there which Sarah now fetched. Then she got to work, butchering her sister right there on the bed, hacking off her arms and then sawing through her midriff. By the time she was done, the room resembled a slaughterhouse. Now Sarah started stuffing Stevie's body parts into black garbage bags which she hauled down to a freezer in the basement. There they were crammed into a large icebox which was then sealed with duct tape. That done, Sarah returned to the bedroom to begin the cleanup.

Sarah Mitchell does not appear to have been the brightest of individuals. Every idea she came up with seemed to surface new problems. One look at the gory mess and Sarah's inner slacker kicked in. The bedroom was literally drenched in blood. It covered the walls, the ceiling, the bedclothes; it had splattered the drapes and the furnishings; it had seeped into the mattress and into the carpet. Cleaning this up was going to take time and elbow grease, and Sarah was not prepared to expend either. Instead, she had another brainwave. It necessitated another trip to the basement. Sarah had spotted a canister of kerosene down there.

The fire was (to Sarah's mind) her most brilliant idea yet. She was well aware of her sister's one-woman anti-drug campaign, aware also that she had pissed off some of the local dealers. There had, in fact, been two arson attempts on the property in the last year. The police would probably think that this was another attempt, a successful one this time. It was the perfect cover.

Sarah had also concocted a plan for concealing her sister's death. She was going to assume Stevie's identity. That would give her the added benefit of being able to clean out Stevie's bank accounts and max out her credit cards. There was also an impending pension payment, due to Stevie from her former employer. This was turning out to be quite a profitable crime.

Unfortunately, Sarah's genius plan did not account for her own incompetence. While setting the blaze, she accidentally lit herself on fire, suffering serious burns to her arms and face. She might well have perished had firefighters not arrived to pull her from the burning house. They were too late to save the property, though. It burned to the ground.

In the aftermath of the fire, Sarah (now posing as Stevie) was heralded as a hero. Recovering in the hospital, she received cards, gifts and donations from well-wishers. There was also outrage in the community that drug dealers could have attacked this brave citizen activist. Pressure was applied to the police, and a $50,000 reward was offered for the apprehension of the culprits. The story even made the front page of several local papers.

And that was bad news for Sarah. After her picture appeared in the media, a relative called the newspaper to set the record straight. The woman depicted in the photograph wasn't Stevie Allman, it was Sarah Mitchell. That information was passed on to the police and an investigation was launched. The main question it needed to answer was: Where was the real Stevie Allman? The answer lay in a sealed icebox in the basement of her destroyed house. The grisly remains were discovered there the very next day. In that moment, Sarah Mitchell went from drug-fighting heroine to savage, heartless killer.

Sarah Mitchell went on trial at the Alameda County Superior Court in November 2000, with the prosecution making its intentions clear right from the start. This was a murder for financial gain and thus met the criteria for the death penalty. If the DA had his way, Mitchell was going to end up strapped to a gurney with a needle in her arm. When

the jury pronounced her guilty as charged, it seemed that it would
indeed end that way.

Fortunately for Mitchell, she had relatives who were disposed towards
forgiveness. Despite her horrific murder of one of their own,
Mitchell's aunt and sister took the stand during the penalty stage to
plead for her life. And their tearful testimonials clearly struck a chord
with the jurors. They returned with a recommendation of life behind
bars with no possibility of parole.

Kelly Silk

Some called it a devout Christian congregation. Others said that the
Truth Baptist Church in South Windsor, Connecticut, was a cult.
Either way, Charles and Kelly Silk were devoted members. The Silks
lived in a handsome colonial revival style house in neighboring East
Hartford. They had four children. The oldest, 8-year-old Jessica, was
Kelly's daughter from an earlier relationship. The other three were all
toddlers – Jennifer, two-and-a-half years of age; Jonah, 17 months; and
Joshua, just two months old. Charles worked for a printing company;
Kelly was a stay-at-home mom. She also home schooled Jessica.

To those looking from the outside in, the Silks were a happy family
whose life centered around their church. Charles was the more devout
of the two, but Kelly was very active in the community. One cause that
was particularly close to her heart was a feeding scheme for the
elderly. Those who knew her said that she was an upbeat person,
devoted to God, to her family, and to good works.

But the Kelly Silk that these people saw was far removed from the real
person. She suffered from acute depression, a symptom perhaps of her
traumatic childhood. When Kelly was just 7 years old, her mother
committed suicide and it was Kelly who found the body, submerged in
a tub of water. As an adult, those memories continued to haunt her,
particularly after the birth of each of her children. She suffered badly
with postpartum depression, with the symptoms at their worst after
Joshua was born in April 1999. With four demanding children to care
for and with the family also overstretched financially, Kelly Silk was
barely clinging on.

And so, Kelly did what her faith demanded of her. Rather than consult a doctor for the treatment that she undoubtedly needed, she spoke to her pastor. He gave her the same advice that he typically delivered from the pulpit at Truth Baptist Church. Doctors couldn't help her; she was to put her trust and faith in the Lord. She was to pray and ask for his guidance and mercy. With this misguided piece of counsel, the seeds of a terrible tragedy were sown.

It was the night of June 10, 1999, and everyone in the Silk household was asleep – everyone, bar two. Joshua was awake and he was crabby; Kelly was awake and she was pacing up and down beside the baby's crib, struggling with her symptoms. Over the prior few days, Kelly had taken her pastor's advice. She'd prayed hard and frequently, begging God to deliver her from the darkness that had enveloped her life. But no help had come, and now Kelly was desperate. After days of soul searching, she'd reached the conclusion that there was only one way out, the way that her mother had chosen. Kelly was about to tread the same path. She was checking out of this life, but she wasn't going alone.

We can't say for sure what it was that eventually pushed Kelly Silk over the edge. What we do know is that, sometime after midnight, Kelly went downstairs, visiting the kitchen and the garage. When she returned to the master bedroom she was carrying a large kitchen knife and a canister of gasoline. The latter, she set aside. The former, she grasped in her hand as she approached the sleeping form of her husband. Charles Silk was awakened by the searing pain of the blade being driven into his back. He suffered several more wounds before he was able to free himself from the blankets and from the frenzied attack. "What are you doing?" he screamed at Kelly as he stumbled to his feet. But then Kelly was on him again, stabbing and slashing. Despite being bigger and heavier than his wife, Charles never stood a chance.

Down the hall, the ruckus had awoken eight-year-old Jessica. Rising bleary-eyed from her bed, the little girl decided to investigate and walked down the passage to her parents' room. She was barely able to comprehend what she saw there. Her mom, wild-eyed and bloodied, straddling her dad, driving a knife into him, again and again. "Mom! Don't!" she cried, but that only served to alert the monster who had taken on her mother's form. Kelly leapt to her feet and crossed the room in a couple of strides. She thrust the knife at her daughter and felt it sink in, withdrew the blade and stabbed again, continuing the attack even as Jessica screamed for her to stop. Over sixty stab and slash wounds were inflicted on the child, leaving her a bloodied mess on the carpet.

And the horror was only just getting started. Kelly now cast the knife aside and went to retrieve the gas canister. Removing the lid, she upended the container, dousing herself and her daughter with gasoline. As the sickly-sweet stench pervaded the room, she lit a match and was instantly engulfed in a fireball. Jessica was burning, too, and that sparked her into action. Miraculously, none of Jessica's multiple wounds had caused a fatal injury. With her hair ablaze, she sprang to her feet and ran, down the stairs, out of the front door and across the road.

Chad Prigge was the Silks' neighbor and also an assistant pastor at their church. It was around 1:30 a.m. when he was roused by a child's screams. Instantly awake, he jumped from his bed and ran to his front door. Throwing it open, he was met by the improbable sight of a little girl on his front lawn, her hair and clothes ablaze. Prigge acted fast, shouting for his wife to bring a blanket and then rushing to Jessica, instructing her to drop to the ground and roll. While she was doing that, Sara Prigge arrived with the blanket and a jug of water, which helped douse the flames. Across the road, the fire had started to take hold of the Silk residence. While Sara Prigge attended to Jessica, her husband ran back inside to call 911.

Jessica Silk was rushed to Connecticut Children's Medical Center in Hartford. Miraculously, given the knife attack and her mother's attempt to burn her alive, she would survive her ordeal, albeit with scars both mental and physical. For the other members of the Silk family, for Kelly, Charles, Jennifer and Jonah, there would be no escape. Charles died of his knife wounds, Kelly of burns and asphyxiation, Jennifer and Jonah of smoke inhalation. But a miracle occurred in the Silk residence that night. Little Joshua was found alive, suffering the effects of smoke and with bruises on his neck, but alive. He would later make a full recovery.

In the aftermath of the murder/suicide, there were many questions to be answered, not least what was to become of the surviving children. Jessica would ultimately be placed in the care of her biological father, but there would be a protracted legal battle for the custody of Joshua. Charles Silk had stipulated in his will that he wanted the Prigge family to raise his children in the event that he and his wife died. However, the Connecticut Department of Children and Families blocked the proposed adoption, stating that bequests relating to the wellbeing of a child are not legally enforceable.

Joshua was placed, instead, with a foster family, leading to the Prigges filing a suit which was ultimately unsuccessful. Part of the reason for the ruling may be the doctrine preached by Truth Baptist Church. The church encourages the corporal punishment of children, for example. As is evident in this case, it also favors prayer over traditional medicine. Had that not been the case, had Kelly Silk been encouraged to seek the treatment she needed, then this tragedy might well have been averted.

Joyce Chant

The story of Joyce Chant is, regrettably, an all too familiar one in modern society. Joyce was a suburban housewife from Sydney, Australia, the mother of three sons, married to a monster. Wayne Chant was a drunkard and a coward, a savage, brutal man who got his kicks beating up his wife and children. For Joyce, this mistreatment had become a fact of life, the way it was, the way it would always be. Wayne would arrive home drunk at night and start on her, criticizing her appearance and her way of running the household. Any effort to defend herself would result in a backhand; further protest would encourage him to use his fists and, often, his boots, if she fell to the ground. It was a terrible way to live.

But the horrific and frequent abuse that Wayne Chant was inflicting on his wife was having an effect. After years of suffering at his hands, Joyce had become hardened. No longer would she meekly submit. Over time, she began to stand up to him, verbally at least, and damn the consequences. Wayne's response was to act out in ever more violent ways, and still Joyce would not "hold her tongue and take her punishment" as he demanded. Eventually, he resorted to death threats, and one night in September 1992, he fetched his rifle from a closet to show that he meant business. That was a mistake.

At the sight of the gun, years of pent-up hate and anger exploded from Joyce. She grappled with Wayne for the weapon. Wayne was stronger but he was drunk and Joyce had the might of righteous fury on her side. When Wayne slipped and started going down, she yanked the weapon from his grip. Now here he was, her lifelong tormentor, cowering on the floor as she shouldered the weapon and stared down the length of the barrel at him. She now had a decision to make, and she took it decisively. "Don't," Wayne uttered. In response, Joyce tightened her finger on the trigger and planted a bullet in the center of his forehead. In the lounge, in front of the TV, the couple's three boys heard a single shot and continued watching their program. They had long ago learned to keep their distance when their parents were fighting.

Over the next few days, an uncharacteristic silence pervaded the Chant household. If the boys wondered about it or about the sudden absence of their father, they broached no questions. They also steered well clear of their parents' bedroom, perhaps fearful of what they'd find there. Had their curiosity drawn them inside, they would have seen a shape wrapped in a sheet, with dried blood smeared on the fabric in the area of the head. That was their father, laid out on the floor beside the bed where their mother slept at night. He would remain there for nearly two weeks, even as the putrefying stench of decomposition invaded the house like a malevolent spirit. Only one person inquired about Wayne Chant's whereabouts during this time. His mother, Dorothy, called at the house several times, demanding to see him. Joyce told her that Wayne had run off with another woman and sent her packing with a few choice words.

Thirteen days had now passed since the death of Wayne Chant, and the stench had become so bad that Joyce was eventually forced into action. One moonless night, after her children had gone to bed, she dragged the corpse out into the backyard. Then she fetched an ax. The first few blows were tentative, but soon that familiar rage had engulfed her, and she was swinging with force and accuracy. Wayne's hands, arms, legs, and head were hacked off, leaving behind the stump of his torso. Joyce's procrastination in disposing of the body had an inadvertent benefit. The blood had congealed and there was no spatter. Within the space of an hour, the butchered corpse was ready for disposal.

Over the next few weeks, a number of macabre discoveries would be recorded at remote locations in and around Sydney. The first of these was made by an unfortunate driver who stopped for a smoke at a rest stop south of the city and stumbled on a dismembered human torso. Then there was a leg and an arm, found separately in wooded areas. The body parts would continue to show up, all except the head and hands, making identification impossible in those pre-DNA days. Dental records or fingerprints were required to solve the mystery, but the body parts that held that information would never be found. They had been placed in an ice cooler, encased in concrete and buried at a separate location by Joyce and her oldest son, James. We don't know why Joyce involved her son in this final act of disposal. Perhaps it was to show him that she had "taken care of business." In any case, it would turn out to be a bad decision.

Years passed, with Joyce continuing to tell her story about Wayne running off with another woman and abandoning her and the children. Knowing the character of the man, most of their friends and relatives were prepared to accept this. But not Dorothy Chant. She remained convinced that Joyce knew something about Wayne's disappearance and continued to pester the police, urging them to treat the case as a murder inquiry. With no evidence of foul play, the police declined to do so.

The murder of Wayne Chant might well have turned out to be the perfect crime had his son Jamie not begun to be plagued by the prickling of a guilty conscience. In 2007, Jamie confessed to a

girlfriend that his mother had murdered his father and that he had
helped her to dispose of the body. He swore the girl to silence, and she
kept her word until they broke up, months later. Then she walked into
a police station and told what she knew. It did not take long for the
police to link her story to the 15-year-old cold case of the Sydney
torso.

Before the police could take any action, however, they had to establish
beyond doubt that the body parts were the remains of Wayne Chant.
But there was a problem. Chant's only living blood relatives were his
three sons, and they did not want to approach them for a comparative
sample since doing so would alert Joyce. Then one of the officers
remembered a peculiarity about the case. Dorothy Chant had died
several years earlier but had insisted before her passing that police take
blood and tissue samples from her. That way, they would have
something for comparison should they ever find Wayne's body. Even
from beyond the grave, she was determined to get justice for her son.

Thus it was that biological material from the unidentified torso, along
with blood and tissue from the now deceased Dorothy Chant were sent
to the top DNA testing facility in the United States. When the results
were returned, they reported a match. Shortly thereafter, the police
arrived at Joyce Chant's Revesby home and took her into custody,
charging her with first-degree murder.

Chant would plead not guilty to murder at her trial but guilty to
manslaughter and to improperly interfering with human remains. She
claimed that she had acted in self-defense when she shot her husband.
Also entered as evidence was testimony regarding the brutal treatment
Joyce and her sons had suffered at the hands of Wayne Chant. James

Chant, now 37 years old, testified that his father had once broken his jaw in two places. He spoke of another incident when his father had rammed his finger into his mother's eye, almost blinding her.

No one in the courtroom was particularly outraged when the jury accepted Joyce's manslaughter plea and sentenced her to just five years in prison. James Chant was acquitted as an accessory.

Nicole Diar

In 1979, when Nicole Diar was four years old, her brother was goofing around with a cigarette lighter and accidentally lit her nightgown on fire. The resulting blaze would have devastating effects for the little girl. She suffered disfiguring burns over 70-percent of her body, injuries which would require sixty-one separate surgeries over the next 14 years. During that time, Nicole's life was one of physical and mental torment. She was shamed by her physical appearance, cut off from her peers, teased by her classmates, who called her "Freddy Krueger." The substantial out-of-court settlement that her family received from the manufacturer of the unintentionally flammable garment was scant compensation for her anguish.

Still, Nicole was a resolute child and grew to be a determined young adult. In her teens, she volunteered with various fire departments to promote safety programs and became a counselor at a camp for children who had suffered injuries similar to hers. Here, she was lauded as a compassionate, caring individual who helped these kids cope with the stigma of their injuries, and with the teasing and taunting they had to endure.

But there was another side to Nicole, one that emerged as she entered her twenties. She liked to party and could be found most nights, trawling the bars and karaoke joints of Lorain, Ohio. This attracted a whole new bunch of friends, all too willing to leech off the $3,000 per month settlement that Nicole received as compensation for her injuries. Add to that a quarterly lump sum payment, and Nicole was flush with cash and generous with it. After being a pariah all of her life, she was suddenly relishing her role as Ms. Popularity. It felt good to receive all of the attention, especially from men.

In 1998, Nicole was delighted to find that she was pregnant. She wasn't exactly sure who the father was, but that didn't matter. All of her life she had believed that she could not have children. Now she was going to be a mom! When her son, Jacob, was born in 1999, she called him her 'miracle baby' and swore that she would be the 'best mom ever.'

And for a time, Nicole lived up to that billing. However, the glow quickly began to fade as the realities of motherhood set in. Being a single mom was a lot more work than she'd anticipated. Moreover, it required sacrifices. No longer could she spend her nights drinking and partying with her buddies. She was back to where she started, isolated from the world, an outcast. And so, Nicole came up with a solution to her problem. She took to doping her son, knocking him out with a combination of codeine and acetaminophen. Then, with the toddler sedated, she'd hit the town, visiting her favorite haunts, reconnecting with her old friends.

Of course, feeding a baby such a powerful cocktail of drugs has consequences. Jacob started suffering with stomach problems, nausea and vomiting. His behavior also swung wildly between lethargy and hyperactivity. This cramped Nicole's style even more, and so she came up with a new plan. She now started hiring local teenagers to look after the child. This was no traditional babysitting arrangement. She would normally allow her childminders to bring their friends over, and there would often be an impromptu party, with booze and cigarettes supplied by Nichole. "If the kid gets on your nerves," she'd tell the minders, "Give him some of this." She'd then hand over her special bottle of knockout drops.

It should be no surprise, given this reckless brand of parenting, that Jacob Diar developed behavioral issues. The little boy became extremely clingy with his mother and never wanted to let her out of his sight. This even extended to bedtime, when he refused to sleep in his own room and insisted on sharing Nicole's bed. This, as you might imagine, had a stifling effect on Nicole's party lifestyle and made her ever more resentful of her son. Jacob was cramping her style. In August of 2003, she decided to do something about it.

At around 9 a.m. on August 27, 2003, firefighters were called to a blaze at 910 West 10th Street in Lorain. They arrived to find thick black smoke billowing from the building and a group of bystanders standing on the sidewalk. One of them was the householder, Nicole Diar, who frantically informed the firefighters, "My baby's inside!" Two firemen then entered the building and headed upstairs, where the anxious mother had told them her son had been sleeping. However, a search of the area failed to turn up the boy. The firefighters then tried going back down, to search the lower floor, but the blaze was now so fierce that they could not make it. They were eventually forced to escape the house by jumping from an upper window.

It would be another hour before the fire was brought under control. Then firefighters were again able to enter, this time searching the lower floor. It was in the main bedroom that they found the remains of Jacob Diar. The little boy had been burned beyond recognition. In fact, the heat had been so intense that it had fused his body to the steel bedframe. He was found clutching the puppy that his mother had bought him just days earlier.

Informed of her son's death, Nicole Diar was remarkably calm, which firefighters put down to shock. She was taken to one of the ambulances to be examined by a paramedic who gave her the all clear. She was then questioned by Detective David Garcia of the Lorain Police Department. According to Nicole, she had been sleeping on the couch in the living room and had woken around 8:50 a.m. to find the house filled with choking black smoke. She'd then gone looking for her son, growing increasingly frantic when she failed to locate him. Eventually, she'd been driven from the building by the noxious fumes, but she'd gone in again after catching her breath. This time she'd lasted only a few seconds before the smoke overcame her and she started hacking and could not go on. When she emerged a second time, her neighbor was in the yard and told her that he had already called 911. The neighbor then tried to enter the house, but he, too, was driven back by the smoke and heat.

Although this appeared a compelling account and was backed up by Nicole's neighbor, the detective had his doubts. Something about the story just did not ring true to him, and he would soon have evidence to back up his suspicions. For starters, there were the statements given by firefighters and paramedics. According to them, Nicole had had no soot on her clothes or body and had not smelled of smoke, as she surely would have, had she been inside the burning house.

And then there were the misleading directions that Nicole had given to the firefighters who'd entered the building to look for Jacob. She'd been insistent that her son was upstairs, and this made sense, since his bedroom was on the upper floor. But as Det. Garcia was to learn from Nicole's friends and relatives, Jacob never slept in his own bedroom and always insisted on sleeping downstairs with his mother. Why then had Nicole been so adamant that he was upstairs? Was it to deliberately mislead the rescuers?

Perhaps, but that still did not amount to solid evidence, at least not evidence that would stand up in a court of law. Far more compelling was the fire investigator's report which stated that an accelerant had been used to ignite the blaze. It was also revealing that the fire had started in the master bedroom, where Jacob just happened to be sleeping. Maybe that was coincidence, but homicide investigators seldom believe in such a thing. One more solid piece of evidence was needed to close the net on Nicole Diar. It came in the form of the pathologist's report.

Jacob's body had been badly charred in the fire, but his internal organs remained intact and revealed one irrefutable fact. The little boy had not died in the blaze. The lack of smoke in his lungs proved that he had already been dead when the fire started. Most likely, it had been set to cover up the true cause of his death. That cause remains a mystery to this day, but investigators can speculate. Based on a tubful of water found in the destroyed house, they believe that Nicole Diar may have drowned her infant son.

Nicole Diar was arrested and charged with first-degree murder within days of her son's death. She continued to protest her innocence right into the trial, with supporters contending that she had loved Jacob and was devastated by his death. The evidence, however, said different. In fact, the prosecution put a number of witnesses on the stand who testified that Nicole had been out drinking and line dancing on the night of Jacob's funeral. "I buried my boy today," she'd told the bartender of the establishment. That is hardly the behavior of a grief-stricken mother.

In the end, the jury took just four hours to convict Nicole Diar of murder. She was sentenced to death in November 2005, although that sentence was later overturned due to a procedural error. In 2010, Diar was moved from Death Row into the general prison population. Now serving life without parole, she continues to insist that she was wrongly convicted.

Regina & Margaret DeFrancisco

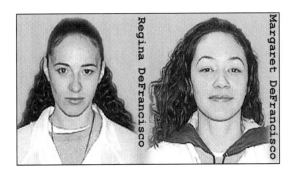

Growing up in one of Chicago's rougher neighborhoods, 22-year-old Oscar Velasquez could quite easily have taken a wrong turn in life. Many of his childhood friends had followed that path, joining one of the local gangs and getting involved in drug dealing and street crime. But Oscar was different; raised in a loving family, he'd stayed in school, stayed off the streets, and eventually graduated. Then he'd got himself a job as a truck driver. He was making good money and doing well. When, in May 2000, he started dating an attractive 17-year-old named Regina DeFrancisco, it seemed that life could hardly get any better.

What Oscar didn't know was that his new girlfriend was playing him. At the time, she had another beau, a local gang member who went by the street name 'Loco'. Loco was currently in the county lockup, awaiting trial on an assault rap. Regina needed $1,000 to bail him out, an amount she didn't have and which she had no way of earning. Her solution to the problem was to seduce Oscar and to scam the money out of him. About a week after he started seeing Regina, Oscar received a call from her little sister, Margaret. According to the 16-

year-old, Regina had been falsely accused of a crime and had been arrested. She was currently in jail and would remain there unless someone put up $1,000 bail. Would Oscar be prepared to help?

Oscar, of course, said yes. What else was he going to do? That same day, he handed over a pile of bills to Margaret and received assurances that it would be paid back within the next few days. Oscar waved those assurances away. "The most important thing is that Regina is safe," he told Margaret.

What Oscar didn't know was that his act of kindness was about to lead him into a world of pain. With Loco back in circulation, Regina started to avoid him, dodging his calls, not answering the door when he came knocking. Then Oscar did some digging and found out that his "girlfriend" was actually dating someone else. That was when he started pressing both Regina and Margaret for the return of his $1,000. Over the next three days, he made as many as 24 calls to the DeFrancisco residence. All but the last of these was met with stonewalling, delaying tactics, and outright lies.

Then, on June 6, 2000, Oscar finally got a commitment out of Regina. She had his money, she said. He could collect it at her house that evening. She also said that she was sorry for the problems she'd caused and wanted to make it up to him. She suggested that sex might be involved. She even hinted that there might be a threesome on offer, also involving her little sister.

Oscar arrived at the DeFrancisco residence at around 8:00 p.m. that evening. He was met at the door by a smiling Margaret who told him that Regina was waiting for him in the basement. Under different circumstances, this might have seemed odd to Oscar, but he was thinking about the potential sexual encounter, blinded to the possibility of a trap. He headed downstairs as instructed, with Margaret behind him. A large sheet of plastic had been laid out on the concrete floor, but Oscar thought nothing of it. He was focused on Regina, who was standing on the other side of the room, a come-hither smile on her face. Oscar smiled back. He was about to say something when Margaret stepped up behind him, raised a pistol and pumped a bullet into his brain at point-blank range.

Oscar collapsed to the floor, blood spouting from the head wound onto the plastic, which had been placed there specifically for that purpose. Upstairs, a friend of the sisters, Veronica Garcia, heard the shot and came rushing down. It was Garcia's gun that Margaret had used in the shooting. She'd borrowed it, telling her friend that she wanted to use it in a holdup. Now, Garcia could see, it had been employed in a far more serious crime.

Oscar was on the ground, blood seeping from his ears and from a gaping head wound. Regina was kicking him and stomping his head (to make him die faster, she'd later tell her friend). Then, with their victim apparently dead, the sisters began stripping the body of valuables, taking Oscar's cellphone, car keys, a gold chain, a handgun, and a wallet containing just over $600 in cash. This they split between them. They then enlisted Garcia's help to wrap their victim in a bedsheet and in the plastic sheeting. Oscar was dragged upstairs, through the house and to his white Camaro Z28. He was manhandled into the trunk of the car.

Later that night, a 911 dispatcher received a report of a fire in a vacant lot in Pilsen, a neighborhood on Chicago's Lower West Side. Firefighters responded to the call and were shocked to find that the blaze was actually a burning body. With the fire quickly brought under control, the police were called and the area cordoned off as a crime scene. One of the first clues they found was a discarded nail varnish remover bottle, the contents of which had been used as an accelerant.

Oscar Velasquez would remain in the morgue for two days as a John Doe. Then police found his car, abandoned on a nearby lot, burned but not entirely destroyed. Linking the two fires, detectives began to piece the puzzle together. It was left to Oscar's parents to perform the terrible task of identifying their son's badly charred remains. They had dedicated their lives to keeping their son away from gang activity and its associated violence. He had fallen victim to violent crime anyway.

This was not a difficult case to crack. In the two days since the murder, the DeFrancisco sisters had offered Oscar's car for sale to several individuals living in the area. They'd also tried to sell his handgun. That made them obvious suspects, but when officers arrived to question them, they found that the sisters had disappeared. A search warrant was then obtained for the residence and turned up plenty of incriminating evidence, including blood in the basement and a pair of pillow cases that exactly matched the sheet the murder victim had been wrapped in. Then the police got an even bigger break. Veronica Garcia came forward to tell what she knew about the crime. Despite her cooperation, she was arrested and charged as an accomplice.

But the two main suspects remained at large and would continue to do so for the next two years. During that time, the case was featured on

both Unsolved Mysteries and America's Most Wanted. It was the
latter show that eventually provided the breakthrough. After a
screening in March 2002, police received a tip that Margaret
DeFrancisco was living with relatives in Rockford, Illinois. She was
arrested on March 24, 2002. Regina's arrest would come seven months
later, on October 18, when she was pulled over in a routine traffic stop
in Dallas, Texas. She then tried to flee, engaging officers in a high
speed chase before she was eventually cornered. She was arrested at
the scene and later extradited to Illinois to stand trial for murder.

Facing an almost unbreakable prosecution case against them, the
DeFrancisco sisters nonetheless entered "not guilty" pleas, claiming
that they had acted in self-defense. At their July 2004 trial, Margaret
claimed that she had entered the living room to find Oscar standing
over her sister, shouting and cussing about the money she owed him.
Oscar was holding a gun on Regina, who was curled up on the floor in
a fetal position begging for her life. Margaret was afraid that her sister
would be killed. She'd therefore drawn her own gun and fired at
Oscar.

The problem with this story was that it was in conflict with the
physical evidence. The police already knew that Oscar had been shot
in the basement. They also knew, via the testimony of Veronica
Garcia, the circumstances of his death. Once Garcia took the stand, the
sisters' fate was effectively sealed.

Regina was ultimately convicted of first degree murder and sentenced
to 35 years in prison. In the case of Margaret, justice would take a
more convoluted path. One hold-out juror refused to vote for
conviction, resulting in a mistrial. The juror apparently refused to

believe that a person so young was capable of cold-blooded murder. Margaret's second jury, however, had no such qualms. She was convicted and received 46 years, eleven years more than her sister. Since it was she who'd fired the fatal shot, it was appropriate that she receive the longer sentence. Her lawyer's pleas for leniency on account of her youth fell on deaf ears.

Regina and Margaret DeFrancisco are currently incarcerated at Dwight Correctional Center in Livingston County, Illinois. They will both be well past middle age by the time they taste freedom. For her role in the murder, Veronica Garcia was sentenced to five years. She has since been released.

Sandy Cain

The year was 1997 and Sandy Greenspan was living in the most vibrant city in the world. Except that New York didn't feel like it held much excitement for Sandy. The 43-year-old dental hygienist was living a life of drudgery, of work and home and family, of a jaded relationship with an abusive husband she no longer cared for. The middle-aged mother-of-one was eager for a new adventure. And since her daughter was now grown and living in her own place, there was nothing holding Sandy back. Nothing, that is, except for her own timid nature.

And so Sandy did what every reticent adventure-seeker does; she took her search for thrills online. A Google search presented her with endless chatrooms for people in her age group. Sandy signed up for a few and dipped her toe in the water. It wasn't long before she was totally immersed in this new and exciting world, chatting to strangers, sharing secrets and experiences. It was in one of these forums that she met Frank Cain.

From the way that he described himself, Frank seemed like the answer to Sandy's prayers, the he-man who would whisk her away into a world of thrills and romance. He was, according to his profile, a bounty hunter living in Las Vegas, Nevada. It didn't hurt either that his picture showed a buff and handsome middle-aged man. Sandy was instantly attracted and decided to make contact. She fired off a message introducing herself and was delighted when she got a response. Soon she and Frank were regular chat buddies. It was then that she learned that Frank's exciting, adventure-filled life went way beyond what she had initially been able to glean about him.

Frank had not always made his living chasing down bail bond defaulters. He'd acquired his detection skills as a CIA agent, working in Thailand and Cambodia during the 1960s. During that time, he confided in Sandy, he had taken out 77 "hostiles." He had commemorated each kill by making a small slash on his body. Not to boast, he said, but to remind himself that he was fulfilling his patriotic duty. He was also an expert in firearms and counter-insurgency, both of which made him very good at his current job and much in demand.

Sandy was fascinated by these stories, more than fascinated. She quickly began developing feelings for Frank, this man she'd never met. It wasn't long before she came to a decision. She needed to be with him. In early 1999, Sandy packed up her things and walked out on her husband. Then she boarded a plane – Destination: Sin City.

Frank was somewhat paunchier than Sandy had imagined, somewhat heavier in the jowl. But that in no way detracted from the way she felt about him. Their first few weeks together were exciting with Frank showing her the sights of Las Vegas and teaching her how to fire a gun. Sandy felt like she was finally living the adventure she had yearned for. When Frank started talking marriage, she was willing to listen. She was even prepared to accede to the strange request he made of her.

This involved signing a "slave contract." According to Frank, he had owned two female slaves while serving in Southeast Asia and could only consider a long-term future with Sandy if similar conditions were in place. The contract would outline their roles in the relationship. Frank would be the master, Sandy the slave. She would cook and clean for him, submit to kinky sex when he demanded it, obey his every command without question. When they were out in public together, she'd walk at least five paces behind him, as befit her status. Bizarre as this arrangement must have seemed, Sandy willingly signed the "contract." She and Frank married in February 1999, once her divorce from her first husband was finalized.

But it was now that Sandy began to learn the true character of her new partner. Far from being the action man that he liked to portray, Frank was a slacker who spent most of his time lying on the couch, drinking beer and watching television. Sandy would come home from work every day to find him passed out in his boxer shorts, amidst a blizzard of empty beer bottles and chip packets. His "thriving" bounty hunter business was non-existent. In fact, he appeared to have no discernible source of income. Not that he needed to work. He had a slave to do that for him now. Sandy was forced to hand her paychecks directly to her "master." Yet even that wasn't enough for him. He also made a habit of maxing out her credit cards.

It did not take long for Sandy Cain to realize that she had made a grave mistake. Her situation in New York had been far from ideal, but at least she'd been her own woman. Now she was little more than a drone. Her life of mundanity had been traded for one of servitude. Still, extricating herself from the situation would have been easy. She could have walked out on Frank and filed for divorce. With her skill set, finding a job would have been easy. She could have started anew somewhere else. But Sandy had been humiliated and taken for a fool. She now doubted everything that Frank had ever told her. A slob like him could never have been in the CIA, and the idea of him chasing down some fugitive seemed ludicrous. Frank had lied to her. He'd manipulated and used her. For that, he was going to have to pay.

On the morning of October 15, 2001, a 911 dispatcher in Las Vegas received an odd call. On the line was a woman, speaking in a whisper, repeating over and over again, "He's going to kill me." Then came the sound of the receiver being put down and, a short while later, five closely spaced gunshots. Then the phone went dead. The operator, of course, called back, and this time the woman on the other end of the line was hysterical, saying that her husband had tried to kill her and that she had shot him in self-defense.

Units were immediately dispatched to the address, where they found Frank Cain lying dead on a couch, the front of his shirt stained red with blood. According to his wife, Sandy, she and Frank had argued about money that morning with the row quickly becoming heated. During the course of the argument, Frank had reached under a couch cushion. Sandy knew that he kept a gun there and thought that he was going for it. She'd therefore grabbed her own 9mm Smith and Wesson and had fired, killing him.

It was a neat enough story, but unfortunately for Sandy, it did not match the forensics. Gunpowder residue was found on the front of Frank's shirt, indicating that he had been shot at very close range, the barrel held no further than a few inches from his chest. The only way that made sense was if Frank was asleep when he was shot. And then there was the 911 call. Investigators believed that Sandy had made the call to back up her claim of self-defense. However, it had the opposite effect. According to Sandy, the couple had been engaged in a furious argument when she made the call. Why then could Frank's voice not be heard, even when the recording was enhanced? The answer was simple. There had been no argument. Frank had been shot while he slept. This was a cold-blooded execution.

Despite sticking to her self-defense story, Sandy Cain was arrested and charged with first-degree murder. But this was a tricky case for both defense and prosecution. There could be little doubt that Sandy had been abused by her husband. A sympathetic jury might take that into account and acquit. On the other hand, the jurors might decide to apply the letter of the law. In that case, the defendant was looking at life in prison without parole. It was no surprise, therefore, when the parties announced that they had struck a deal.

In April 2002, Sandy Cain entered a plea of "no contest" to a charge of second-degree murder. In doing so, she accepted a term of 10 to 20 years, with credit for time served. She would remain behind bars until 2011, when she was released on parole.

Sandy Cain had come to Las Vegas looking to escape her humdrum existence. She headed back east with a new perspective on life. Boredom isn't necessarily the worst thing that a person might be forced to endure.

Antoinette Scieri

The name Antoinette Scieri is all but unknown today. But back in the 1920s, Scieri was one of the most notorious women in France, a female killer who dispatched her victims in agony and for the most insipid of reasons – she simply enjoyed the taking of human life.

Scieri was an Italian national, born in Bologna around 1890. We know nothing at all about her childhood and upbringing, but we do know that she immigrated with her family to France at the turn of the century and worked as a nurse at a field hospital near Doullens during the First World War. Antoinette had no formal training for this vocation, and her motives were less than honorable. She wasn't there to care for the sick and wounded, she was there to rob them. Cash, watches, and other items of value found their way into the pockets of Nurse Scieri's tunic, and she even forged letters to the families of some of the wounded soldiers asking for money. She was eventually caught while lifting an officer's pay book. That earned her a year in prison.

Emerging from her period of incarceration in 1916, Antoinette married an Italian soldier named Salmon, bearing him two children over the next two years. When she became pregnant for a third time, though, Salmon began to suspect that the child might not be his. A little bit of snooping around proved that he was right. His wife had been playing the field. Salmon promptly left, abandoning Antoinette and her brood. Her third child was born out of wedlock. Seeking a new start, she next moved to St. Gilles, a picturesque little village in the south of France, near the historic city of Nimes. She arrived there in 1920 and soon had her hooks in a new lover. Henri Rossignol was the son of a wealthy landowner and somewhat younger than Antoinette. He was considered quite a catch. Antoinette would quickly discover that he was not.

The relationship between Antoinette Scieri and Henri Rossignol was an extremely volatile one. Henri was a heavy drinker, and when he was in his cups, he liked to use his fists, usually on Antoinette. She was hailed around town as somewhat of a saint, just for putting up with him. And that did nothing to hurt her new business venture. In April 1924, she started offering her services as a nurse.

Of course, "Nurse Scieri" held no formal qualification in this field. But she had learned a lot at the military hospital, and what she didn't know, she was able to fake. She also had an exceptional bedside manner. Those who engaged her services said that she watched over them like a mother over a sick child. If they survived, that is. Many of her patients did not. Between April and November alone, five women died under her care. Because they were all elderly and infirm, no one batted an eyelid. At least Nurse Scieri had made their final days comfortable.

But Antoinette was only just getting started. December 1924 was a particularly deadly month. First Marie Drouard, a 58-year-old spinster, died in her care. Then, on Christmas Day, Monsieur and Madame La Chapelle, two of the town's most distinguished citizens, both died, one within three hours of the other. Madame La Chapelle had been afflicted with an abscess of the throat which had made breathing difficult. According to Scieri, she had passed peacefully. Her grief-stricken husband had then suffered a heart attack and had died within hours. A local physician, called in to verify the cause of death, agreed with that assessment. That was a good thing for Scieri because the rumor mill had started to crank. It cranked even louder when Henri Rossignol fell ill just six days later.

Rossignol's symptoms had begun after he consumed a bowl of mussels, prepared for him by Antoinette. Food poisoning was suspected, and Antoinette could not have been more attentive. Still sporting a black eye from her last beating at his hands, she hustled Henri off into bed, made him comfortable and fed him a tonic which she said would alleviate the symptoms. Except that it didn't provide much relief at all. It seemed to make him even more ill. For hours on end, he rolled around in his bed, screaming in agony, periodically throwing up, sometimes soiling himself before he could make it to the bathroom. Then Antoinette would dutifully clean him up, change the bedclothes and tuck him in. For a few hours, Henri would fall into a fitful sleep. Then Antoinette would wake him to take his medicine, and the cycle would begin all over again.

Henri Rossignol would linger in this hellish condition for over two months, his symptoms becoming so severe that at times he prayed for death. During that time, Antoinette seldom left his side, refusing all offers of work. Finally, on March 18, 1925, Henri's body gave in and he passed away. Antoinette was present when he died, and she appeared devastated. Despite Henri's somewhat tarnished reputation, the entire village grieved with her. It was seldom that you saw such devotion between lovers.

Antoinette did not grieve for long. On the day that Henri was laid to rest in the local churchyard, she began caring for Marie Martin, a pretty young thing who was the daughter of the town's leading lawyer. Marie suffered from asthma, which was at its worst in the springtime. Within days of Nurse Scieri's ministrations, she was dead.

Scieri had miscalculated badly, though, in targeting such a young victim. Marie's father demanded an investigation, and preparations began to be made for an exhumation and autopsy. Yet even now, with the law breathing down her neck, Scieri just could not help herself. Her final victim was Madame Gouant, the elderly wife of one of the town's most eminent businessmen. She breathed her last on April 9, 1925, and the authorities then stepped in to close down Nurse Scieri's death factory, once and for all.

The evidence against Antoinette Scieri stacked up pretty quickly after that. First the police found a large bottle of pyralion hidden at her lodgings. This is a derivative of arsenic, commonly used on grapevines as a pesticide. Since St. Gilles is right in the middle of wine country, it was easy to obtain. The quantity found in Scieri's possession was enough to kill a hundred people. The bodies of Henri Rossignol, Marie Martin, and others were brought to the surface. Subjected to autopsy, they were found to be riddled with the deadly toxin. Antoinette Scieri was then charged with a dozen murders.

But the homicidal nurse was not about to take these charges lying down. While awaiting trial, she implicated Rosalie Gire, a village woman who she had contracted to help her care for her patients. According to Scieri, Gire was well-versed in the effects of different poisons. It was Gire who had suggested pyralion, saying that it acted as a sedative when given in the right dosage. "I tried this several times, and it always worked in alleviating pain," Scieri insisted. "I had no idea that the effect was cumulative. Gire didn't warn me."

In essence, Scieri was pleading accidental death while at the same time dropping Rosalie Gire in deep water. Gire was soon arrested but just as quickly dismissed as a suspect. She was a simple village woman, quite naïve, and easily manipulated by the likes of Scieri. There was nothing to suggest that she had even the slightest knowledge of poisons.

Naming Rosalie Gire as a murder suspect would come back to haunt Antoinette Scieri. Gire might not have known anything about pyralion, but she was able to provide the police with a disturbing description of Henri Rossignol's final moments. Rossignol's death was the most protracted of any that Scieri caused. He was made to suffer for months before the killer nurse finally put him out of his misery. This makes sense because Rossignol's murder was personal. He had battered Antoinette one time too many and would pay a dreadful price for the abuse he inflicted on her.

According to Gire, she had decided to go to Antoinette's house on the night that Henri Rossignol died. She was not expected but knew that Antoinette had been tending the sick man all day and reckoned that she must be exhausted. She only wanted to help. She was not prepared for the sight that greeted her on arrival.

Rossignol was lying on the bed, gasping for breath, his body racked periodically by spasms. Meanwhile, Antoinette was seated at a table next to the dying man. On it was a feast that included a roasted pheasant, truffles, a bottle of champagne and other delicacies. Antoinette was digging in, enjoying some kind of celebration. Then she got up, leaned over Rossignol, and stared intently into his eyes. She appeared, according to Gire, to be in a state of ecstasy. When Gire interrupted and asked her about the macabre banquet, Antoinette told her that she had fixed herself a "snack" because she was near collapse after tending Henri for three days and three nights.

Rosalie Gire would repeat this story during the trial. Along with the physical evidence, it painted a damning picture of Antoinette Scieri. It was no surprise when Scieri was found guilty on April 27, 1926, and sentenced to die by guillotine. "You have been called a monster," the judge said during his summation, "but that is not a strong enough word. You are debauched. You are possessed of all the vices. You are a vicious drunkard and a hypocrite. You have no shame. I do not believe judicial history contains the records of many criminals of your type."

If those words were intended to wound the defendant, they missed their mark by some distance. Scieri seemed amused by the whole thing. Hearing her death sentence, she simply shrugged her shoulders and chuckled, assuring the judge that she would not be executed.

And that prediction turned out to be accurate. The French judiciary had little taste for lopping the heads off women, no matter how debauched. Not a single female had been guillotined since the end of World War I and Antoinette Scieri would not break that trend. Her sentence was commuted to life in prison. She subsequently died behind bars.

Kelly O'Donnell

On the morning of November 13, 1992, Philadelphia police received a report of a gruesome discovery on North Delaware Avenue. Officers responded to the scene and found human body parts – the severed arms of a white male, a headless torso, and a head that had suffered severe trauma and from which the left eye had been removed. The corpse had also been emasculated and the penis was missing. Also, there was no trace of the victim's legs.

Later that night, at around 7:30 p.m., Philadelphia PD officers were summoned to the scene of another crime. A car was ablaze on D Street, the fire apparently set on purpose. Firefighters quickly got the blaze under control, and it was then that the police established a link to their earlier crime scene. The victim's severed legs were found inside the vehicle. Now, at least, investigators had an ID on their John Doe. The car was registered to Eleftherios Eleftheriou, a 50-year-old pizza parlor owner known locally as "Terry the Greek." The question was, who had killed him? And why?

One valuable clue was a letter that had been found inside one of the garbage bags containing the dismembered remains. It was addressed to a woman named Agnes McClinchey, who lived at 3123 Richmond Street. Detectives had called on the apartment that morning but had found no one home. Now, with the discovery of the burned-out car and yet more body parts, they were about to make a follow-up call. Before they could do that, Agnes McClinchey contacted them, asking to meet at a gas station near her home. She had a very interesting story to tell.

According to McClinchey, she had returned to her apartment on the afternoon of November 13, after visiting with friends for a few days. On arriving, she had spotted a small patch of blood near the front door and more of the stuff soaked into a hallway carpet. Her son, William Gribble, had been staying in the apartment while she was away, and so she had asked him about the stain. However, it wasn't William who answered, but his girlfriend, Kelly O'Donnell. And what Kelly had to say was shocking. She said that she and William had murdered somebody in the apartment. "But you shouldn't worry," she'd added with a chuckle, "We got rid of the body."

McClinchey had been certain that Kelly was joking. But then she'd seen the news report of human remains found on Delaware Avenue. A short while later, she'd heard Kelly tell William to "burn the car," warning him not to get caught. That was when she realized that Kelly had been deadly serious. While William was out of the apartment, she had made an excuse to go out and had then walked to the gas station, from where she'd called the police.

Police work, as any detective will tell you, relies heavily on tip-offs. And this was as credible a tip as the police were ever likely to get.

They immediately began planning a takedown of the suspects. At 1:30 a.m. on the morning of November 14, officers carried out a raid on the Richmond Street apartment and took Kelly O'Donnell and William Gribble into custody. The suspects were then transported to police headquarters for questioning. In the meantime, officers carried out a search of the apartment building and hit pay dirt in the basement, where they uncovered a kitchen knife, a chisel, and a claw hammer, all encrusted with blood and smeared with traces of human hair and tissue. They also made a more macabre discovery, a pencil case containing the victim's missing eyeball… and his penis.

With such an overwhelming cache of evidence, the police believed that they would quickly have their case sewn up. Criminal associates often turn on their cohorts when the chips are down, and skilled investigators know just how to play them off against each other. But very little manipulation was required here. In fact, O'Donnell and Gribble seemed eager to take "credit" for the murder themselves, while at the same time exonerating the other. According to O'Donnell, it was she who'd killed Terry the Greek. Gribble had helped only with the clean-up. Gribble told a similar story. Except that in his version of events, he was the killer and O'Donnell was entirely innocent. Unable to sort the lies from the truth, investigators charged them both. In the eyes of the law, they were equally responsible.

So what had happened to Terry the Greek and why was he killed in such a brutal fashion? Since William Gribble claimed that he could remember nothing of the actual murder, it is best to rely on Kelly O'Donnell's account. She recalled every grisly detail and was happy to describe them to the police, sparing none of the blood and gore.

According to Kelly, Terry had been a pervert who'd frequently propositioned her for sex. She had put up with his advances only because she and William frequently borrowed money from him to finance their drug habit. This was the case on the morning of November 11, when Kelly walked to Terry's pizza parlor to ask for a loan of $100. She'd offered him a leather jacket as security, but he'd told her it wasn't necessary since the loan was only for a few hours. His only condition was that she meet with him at her apartment later that night, to settle the debt. Kelly knew what that meant. Terry was going to try his luck with her again. Probably, he'd offer to write off the debt in exchange for sex. Since she needed the money, she agreed to his terms.

In the early morning hours of November 12, Terry Eleftheriou closed up his restaurant and set off to keep his appointment with Kelly. He arrived at around 1:30 a.m. and found Kelly alone, since William had gone out to score some drugs. As Kelly had suspected, he soon began pressing her for sex, advances which she rebuffed by telling him that her boyfriend would be home soon. On this night, however, Terry wasn't taking no for an answer. He pushed her on the issue, getting quite physical. He might well have raped her had he not been distracted by a noise from outside. He'd then gone to the window to investigate, and that was when Kelly picked up a hammer, crept up behind him and struck him on the head. Terry collapsed immediately to the floor, and then Kelly was on him, swinging the hammer in a frenzied attack. She did not stop until his head was a mess of blood, shattered bone, and brain matter.

That part of O'Donnell's story was at least believable. The next part was a stretch. After killing Terry, she claimed that she had dragged him down into the basement, where she had dismembered the body with a hacksaw, placing the body parts in trash bags. While doing so, she'd removed one of his eyes and cut off his penis. She'd done these things, she said, because he was always ogling her and because he'd once masturbated in front of her. She also said that she'd kept the penis because she wanted to mail it to her father, "for a laugh."

There are a number of reasons to question this part of Kelly's account. Kelly wasn't a particularly powerfully-built woman. It seems unlikely that she'd have been able to move the body on her own. And dismembering a corpse with a hacksaw is tough, backbreaking work. It is hard to believe that she could have achieved it, especially given the time frame she was claiming. Nonetheless, Kelly was adamant. William Gribble had only found out about the murder after the fact, when she'd told him about it. The two of them had then spent the day driving around in their victim's car, enjoying a shopping spree on his credit cards. Gribble's only involvement was in helping her dump the body parts.

As for William Gribble's version of events, he claimed that he had returned to the apartment to find Terry the Greek molesting Kelly. He'd then snapped and killed him on the spot. However, he could remember little of the actual murder since he'd been high on booze and drugs at the time. He was at pains to stress, however, that Kelly had had nothing to do with the killing.

Given these conflicting accounts, it is unlikely that we will ever know for certain what happened inside 3123 Richmond that night. However, the specifics are unimportant when it comes to the application of the law. Two individuals acting in concert to commit a murder are equally guilty, regardless of who struck the killing blow. Kelly O'Donnell and

William Gribble were both convicted and sentenced to death. Their sentences were later commuted to life in prison without parole.

Janice Carter

Some marriages are made in heaven. Others are crafted in hell. In the case of Paul and Janice Carter, it was definitely the latter. Paul and Janice had the proverbial on-again-off-again relationship. They'd been together and apart, married and divorced; they had raised two children together but had split countless times over allegations of infidelity and drink-fueled domestic violence. But always, once the dust had settled, one or the other would come crawling back, apologies would be made and accepted, the whole cycle would repeat itself. Whatever the cost in blood and tears, it seemed they just could not stay away from each other.

But in 2011, a split occurred that the couple could not remedy with an apology and some make-up sex. Paul was arrested and sentenced to 180 days in prison for driving offences. The Carters were, at the time, divorced but living together in an apartment on Sweyn Road in Margate, on England's southeast coast. They had been talking about remarrying and having more children, and somehow the prison walls that separated them seemed to intensify their passion. Janice was a regular visitor during Paul's incarceration, and passionate letters passed to and fro between them. When Paul was released on October 14, 2011, Janice was there to collect him.

Given the history of their relationship, it would probably have been advisable for Paul and Janice to take things slow after Paul walked free that day. It would definitely have been wise for them to take it easy on the booze. Instead, the reunited couple found the nearest pub, crept into a booth and started making out like teenagers. They also glugged down several beers, alternating them with shooters. By the time they left the bar, they were both somewhat the worse for drink.

But the party was only just getting started. Back at the apartment, Janice broke out a bottle of Paul's favorite tipple, Southern Comfort, and they toasted his freedom, the troubles they had left behind, and the happy life they were going to have together. They also turned up the stereo, playing their music so loud that their neighbor was soon pounding on the door. Rather than complying with his request to turn it down, they shoved a drink in his hand and invited him in to join the party.

A short while later, the festivities had to be put on hold when employees of the security firm G4S arrived to install a tracking device in the apartment. This was a condition of Paul's parole, and he had been expecting them. However, the location of the tracking unit soon became a bone of contention between Paul and Janice. He wanted it in the bedroom, while she suggested the kitchen. After a heated exchange, Paul's opinion prevailed. The unit went beside the bed and the installers departed, leaving Janice in a huff. Then Paul decided to make a call to his son and got a less than enthusiastic welcome. It was at this point that things started to go awry.

The phone call had an instant effect on Paul's mood. He started stalking from room to room, cursing and kicking things. To Janice, this was a clear warning sign. She knew all about her partner's "Jekyll and Hyde" personality, one minute joyful, the next angry and aggressive. She therefore decided to take precautionary measures and asked the neighbor to pour Paul's full glass of Southern Comfort down the drain. "He won't realize it's gone," she assured the man. "He never does when he gets like this."

But Paul did notice, and it only served to inflame an already volatile situation. He started throwing threats and curses, first at Janice and then at the neighbor. The argument over the tracking unit flared up again and continued with the couple going head-to-head, screaming in each other's faces. Perhaps wisely, the neighbor said his goodbyes and departed. Now the Carters were alone in the apartment, both drunk, both fuming. This could only end badly.

We only have Janice Carter's word for what happened next. According to Janice, Paul started slapping her, delivering meaty blows that rocked her head from side to side. He then grabbed her by the forearms and started screaming in her face. Desperately, she tried to reason with him, tried to calm him down. But Paul was beyond reason. He now let go of her arms and started stalking again, kicking out at anything in his path, sending a side table and several trinkets crashing across the room. Seeing an opportunity, Janice made a dash for the front door, but Paul cut her off, grabbed her by the hair, dragged her into the kitchen. There, he resumed the assault, blows raining down on the helpless woman.

Janice had suffered many beatings at the hands of her partner during their tumultuous years together, but she had never seen him quite as furious as this. Her only thought was that he was going to kill her unless she could get free of him. Reaching across the counter, her hand closed on something, the handle of a large kitchen knife. Without even thinking, she swung, sending the blade on an arc that terminated in her attacker's midriff. She heard him cry out, felt his grip on her hair loosen. But Janice was operating on autopilot now. She kept swinging the blade, withdrawing, thrusting again. She continued even after Paul collapsed to the kitchen floor, bleeding from multiple cuts. The pathologist would later count 21 knife wounds, all of them deep, many of them fatal. Paul's vital organs – heart, liver, lungs – had all been penetrated.

With her ex-husband now dying, bleeding out on the kitchen floor, Janice Carter eventually broke off the attack, dropped the knife and ran. She arrived minutes later at the home of her sister, Michelle Cheney. "I killed him," she said. "I stabbed him. I think he's dead." One look at her sister's blood-spattered clothes and Michelle knew that she wasn't kidding. Nonetheless, she sent her husband to check. It was he who found Paul Carter's butchered corpse, he who called 999.

Arrested and taken in for questioning, Janice Carter made no pretense at innocence. She admitted that she had stabbed her husband but insisted that she had acted in self-defense after suffering years of physical and emotional abuse. She also claimed that it had not been her intention to kill, only to stop Paul from hitting her. That was precisely the defense she put up at her March 2012 trial, held at the Canterbury Crown Court.

But there were several items of evidence that challenged Janice Carter's version of events. The first was the testimony of the neighbor, who had been present when the argument started and had heard the rest of it through the walls, as the couple continued to hurl abuse and curses. According to him, Janice had been far from passive and had stood her ground, sometimes drowning out her ex-husband with her yelling. There was also the autopsy report which suggested a savage attack. If Janice's intention was to free herself, why had she continued stabbing even after Paul had been incapacitated? Why had she not fled after inflicting the first wound?

These were the questions that the eight women and four men of the jury would have to ponder. Was this self-defense (and therefore justifiable homicide), was it manslaughter, or was it murder? The verdict, by a majority of 11-1, was for murder. Judge Adele Williams summed it up best when she described Janice Carter's actions thus: "It started out as a defense but turned into an attack." The judge then sentenced Janice Carter to life in prison with a minimum tariff of 12 years. Janice wept bitterly as the sentence was read.

The real tragedy of this case is that the tragic outcome seems so inevitable in retrospect. Paul and Janice Carter were toxic to one another, a dangerous combination of detonator and dynamite. Every reunion they'd attempted had ended in violent confrontation sooner or later. The final one had lasted mere hours. Paul Carter had walked free from prison on the afternoon of October 14, 2011. By 8:30 that evening, he was dead on the kitchen floor in a pool of his own blood.

Sheila LaBarre

Sheila Kay Bailey was born in July 4, 1958, in Fort Payne, Alabama. We don't know a lot about her childhood other than what she herself would reveal in later years, that she has a sister, Lynn; that she graduated from Fort Payne High School; and most pertinently, that she was sexually abused by her father as a young child. That would instill in Sheila a lifelong hatred of pedophiles, a hatred that would have deadly consequences for at least two young men.

That, however, lay in the future. For now, Sheila was desperate to escape her parental home. So desperate, in fact, that she married the first man who asked her. Ronnie Jennings was (again, according to Sheila) an abusive man who she tried to leave but who refused to give her a divorce. Ronnie, however, tells a different story. He says that his wife, who had by now acquired the nickname "Crazy Sheila" due to her bizarre behavior, often threatened him with violence. He would lie awake at night, afraid to doze off lest she stabbed him while he slept.

Whatever the truth of the matter, the marriage ended in 1980, when Sheila was admitted to a psychiatric facility. She had attempted suicide by overdosing on prescription drugs and then driving her car at high speed into a ditch. While confined to the hospital, she would accuse an orderly of sexual assault, a charge that was investigated but not proven.

But whatever her problems with men, Sheila appeared to enjoy their company. Even before her divorce from Ronnie Jennings was finalized, she was cohabitating with a man named John Baxter. Sheila was 23 years old; Baxter was 19 and had a baby daughter. After the couple wed on New Year's Eve 1981, they set up home together with Sheila taking on the role of homemaker and childminder. That was a mistake. A few weeks into the marriage, John felt ill at work one day and left early. He arrived home to find Sheila lounging on the couch and his little girl locked in a closet. He filed for divorce the next day. The marriage had lasted just six weeks.

We next catch up with Sheila in 1987, when she arrived in Hampton, New Hampshire, to begin a romance with a chiropractor named Wilfred "Bill" LaBarre. LaBarre ran a thriving chiropractic practice in the town. He was well-liked and respected. He was also wealthy. Among his assets was a million-dollar horse ranch in nearby Epping. All of these material possessions, though, could not assuage Bill's loneliness. His wife had recently died, and he was craving female company. He therefore placed an ad in the personal column of a local newspaper. To his detriment, it was "Crazy Sheila" Bailey who answered.

Still, Sheila appears to have been on her best behavior during the early days of their relationship. In fact, she made such a positive impression on Bill that he made her the office manager of his practice. Their mail order romance, however, was short-lived. Sheila wanted marriage, and Bill was less keen on the idea. When things cooled between them, she moved out of his house and into an apartment that Bill owned, above his office in Hampton. While living there, Sheila legally adopted the name LaBarre, much to the chagrin of Bill's daughter, Laura Melisi. Laura didn't trust Sheila and believed that she was after her father's fortune. She had good instincts in that regard.

Over the next few years, the small Hampton police force became well acquainted with Sheila LaBarre. In 1995, Sheila entered into another volatile marriage, this time with Jamaican national Wayne Ennis. Soon the police were dealing with claim and counterclaim of domestic abuse. Sheila asserted that Wayne tried to force her car off the road, punched her in the head, and kicked her. Wayne said that she had attacked him with scissors. He also claimed that she had asked him to kill Bill LaBarre. Unsurprisingly, the union was dissolved within a year.

But Ennis wasn't the only man to suffer at Sheila's hands. She still appeared obsessed with the idea of marrying Bill LaBarre and pestered him constantly to "do the right thing." On one occasion, she even chased Bill down a street in central Hampton, waving a gun. That incident resulted in a restraining order being granted for a year. It succeeded in keeping Sheila at bay during that time but could not keep her out of trouble. In 1998, she was charged with assault after she stabbed her latest paramour in the head with a pair of scissors. Amazingly, the police called the incident a "lover's tiff," and Sheila walked away with no more than a warning.

And then, in 2000, Sheila LaBarre was again the name on everyone's lips. Bill LaBarre died suddenly and left his entire estate – his business, two properties in Somersworth, a house in Portsmouth, and his 115-acre horse ranch in Epping – to Sheila. All told, the estate was worth around $2 million. The fact that Bill had left it all to a woman with whom he'd had a short-term fling, the fact that he had disinherited his own daughter in the process, should have raised suspicions but didn't. Despite rumors that Bill Labarre had been coerced into making the will and then murdered, the police decided not to investigate.

Crazy Sheila moved onto her newly acquired horse ranch and soon made herself known to Epping's law enforcement community. She badgered the police constantly with calls, letters, and personal visits. Her neighbors were trespassing; the road running past her property was dangerous; her latest boyfriend had beaten her up. It got so that local officers dreaded a ringing phone. Any officer who had the misfortune of being sent to the LaBarre farm to investigate a complaint would be subjected to a barrage of sexual harassment. Sheila would expose herself and try to talk the officer into her bed. When he refused, she would become aggressive, launching into one of her bizarre tirades.

There were other incidents, too, in which complaints were lodged against LaBarre rather than by her. James Brackett, the same man she'd stabbed in the head in 1998, was back. In 2002, Brackett complained to police that Sheila had tried to run him down with her car. In 2003, she raked her nails across his face and then fired a gun at him. The result, as always, was a mere slap on the wrist. None of these complaints ever made it into a courtroom.

And perhaps the law's lenient attitude to her misdemeanors emboldened Sheila. She began hanging out at homeless shelters, successfully luring a procession of young men with offers of work on her farm. Except that their duties had less to do with tending the livestock and more to do with performing stud duties in Sheila's bedroom. None of these men stayed very long, and some of them spoke about their treatment at Sheila's hands. They said that she was a sexual sadist who enjoyed tying them up and inflicting pain on them. A number of these men were also seen around town, beaten and bloodied. And they were the lucky ones. For at least two of Sheila LaBarre's harem, the Epping horse ranch would be their last stop on the trail.

The first of those men was 38-year-old Michael Deloge, a developmentally disabled man who LaBarre met at a homeless shelter in 2004. At first, Deloge's mother and stepfather were delighted that he had a job. They also had no objection when he told them that he was involved romantically with his wealthy employer. But then Michael started showing up with cuts and bruises and sometimes walking with a pronounced limp. His mother, Donna, also learned that he had been doing drugs and that he had developed a fascination with sadomasochism. That was when she tried to convince him to break it off. Michael, however, would hear none of it. He said that he loved Sheila and was staying with her. A short while later, Donna received a video cassette in the mail. It was a recording of Michael, making hurtful accusations, claiming that he'd been abused by her as a child. It was followed up by a letter in which he told her that he never wanted to see her again.

Over the weeks that followed, there were several sightings of Michael Deloge, usually by Sheila's neighbors. On each occasion, he looked worse than the time before, covered in cuts, scratches, and bruises. One neighbor found him limping along a road with blood streaming from a cut to his ear. Asked what had happened, Michael said that Sheila had attacked him with scissors. He then made the neighbor promise that he wouldn't say anything.

And then, in the Fall of 2005, Michael Deloge was gone. When his mother asked about him, Sheila said that he had left in the middle of the night and that she had no idea where he was. Donna reported her son missing. The police did not even bother questioning Sheila about it.

In February 2006, Sheila had a new man in her life. Like Michael Deloge, 24-year-old Kenneth Countie was developmentally disabled, with the intellectual capacity of a 12-year-old. That made him easy to control and manipulate. Countie soon took up residence at Sheila LaBarre's ranch, abandoning his Massachusetts home without so much as a word to his mother, Carolynn Lodge. Since the pair were close, Carolynn was concerned and filed a missing person report which brought police officers to the LaBarre ranch. There, they found Kenneth happy and in good health.

That was on February 24, ten days after Ken had set up home with Sheila LaBarre. But the relationship must have gone downhill pretty quickly from there. On March 17, 2006, employees of the Epping Wal-Mart saw an odd couple enter the store. The man was in a wheelchair, his face and arms marked by scratches and bruises, his skin a sickly, ashen hue. The woman who was pushing the chair directed it to the aisle containing plastic gasoline canisters. She pulled several of these from the shelves and stacked them into her companion's lap. Then, as she was turning towards the tills, she got into an argument with another shopper, accusing the man of bumping into her boyfriend's chair. The row quickly escalated, becoming so heated that the police had to be called.

The officers who responded to the scene soon got things under control. It wasn't the argument that bothered them, though, it was the state of the young man in the wheelchair. Ken Countie appeared to be deathly ill and sporting multiple injuries. When an officer asked if he was okay, he made no response, he simply nodded, with his eyes directed to the floor. "He's fine," Sheila LaBarre snapped. "No thanks to the asshole who crashed into him." The cops then warned her and the other shopper to let the matter drop and departed the scene, abandoning Ken Countie to his fate.

A few days after the Wal-Mart incident, Sheila LaBarre showed up at several farms bordering her property and asked if anyone had seen Kenny Countie. She claimed that Countie usually got up early to feed the animals but had not done so this morning and was not on her property. She suspected that he might have taken off during the night. She had, of course, told a similar story when Michael Deloge disappeared.

On March 23, 2006, Carolynn Lodge called the police and reported her son missing. That same day, she called the ranch and spoke to Sheila, who told her that Kenny had returned to Massachusetts. No amount of probing could get Sheila to change her story, and Carolynn was eventually forced to let it drop. At this point, it looked as though Sheila had played her familiar ruse again…and won.

But just a day later, Crazy Sheila pulled a move that was incredibly bizarre, even by her standards. At around 1:00 a.m. on the morning of March 24, she called the Epping police and insisted on playing an audiotape for the officers on duty. It was a recording of her "interrogation" of Kenny. On the tape, Sheila could be heard shouting questions at Ken, accusing him of raping children. Ken can be heard in the background, blubbering that he "did it." In the next moment, he is heard retching violently. Then Sheila's voice is heard again, yelling at him to stop pretending that he has passed out.

The tape made for very disturbing listening and also cast serious doubts on Ken Countie's wellbeing. Yet, incredibly, it would take the Epping police seventeen hours to respond. It was only at 6:00 p.m. the following afternoon that they arrived at the ranch to check on Ken. They did not find him in the home but they did find plenty of evidence that something was not right.

A burned-out mattress lay in the front yard, beside the three gas canisters that Sheila had bought at Wal-Mart. There was also a pile of burning hay and a hunk of bloody bone that looked like it might be human. The officers were inspecting this when Sheila arrived and ordered them to leave. Asked about the bone, she answered sarcastically that it was either "a rabbit or a pedophile." When the officers asked if they could take it away for testing, she flatly refused.

The police were forced to leave empty-handed. But the following day, they were back, and this time they had a search warrant. They found Sheila LaBarre in the kitchen, exhausted, covered in soot, and packing a handgun. She was ordered to hand over the weapon and she meekly complied. Then she told the officers that she had "burned a pedophile."

However, LaBarre would back down from that admission once she was in an interrogation room at the Epping police station. She was now back to telling her original story, saying that Kenny had left the farm after confessing to her that he was a pedophile. He had told her that he intended killing himself. She then handed over a note, supposedly written by Ken Countie. In it, he admitted to his "vile acts against children."

The following day, March 26, officers returned to the LaBarre ranch and continued their search, eventually accumulating a wealth of evidence. There was a blood-caked knife and blood spatters in virtually every room of the house; there was bloody clothing belonging to Michael Deloge; there were several "burn pits" from which were extracted fragments of bone and several human teeth. Some of these were quite old, leaving investigators to wonder – just how many men had died here?

By now, there was little doubt that something bad had happened to Ken Countie on the LaBarre ranch. It was also not a stretch to imagine that there must be might victims. Michael Deloge, certainly, and perhaps others beside. And yet, amazingly, LaBarre was not retained in custody. On March 28, surveillance officers watched as she went into her bank and withdrew over $80,000 in cash. The following day, she evaded them, walked out to the I-293 and stuck out her thumb. By the time an arrest warrant was issued on March 31, she was long gone.

But Sheila LaBarre's flight from justice would be a short one. She was arrested just two days later in Revere, Massachusetts. Under questioning, she denied causing harm to Ken Countie, insisting that she had ended the relationship after he'd confessed to her that he was a pedophile. She had asked him to leave, and he had done so on March 21, hitting the road in the middle of the night. She'd woken the following morning to find him gone. She'd then dragged her mattress outside and burned it because she had "slept on it with a pedophile." She did not know where Ken was, but she had not caused him any harm.

The police, of course, did not believe her, not least because the bone fragments found at the farm had now definitely been identified as human. Sheila LaBarre was therefore charged with the first-degree murder of Kenneth Countie and was denied bail. She then surprised everyone by changing her story and admitting to two murders – Ken Countie and Michael Deloge. She'd killed them, she said, because they were pedophiles, and she was on a mission to rid the world of such creatures. According to Sheila, she had once died but had been sent back to Earth as an angel with special powers and a mission to avenge abused children.

Such flights of fantasy were, of course, typical of Crazy Sheila. And given her history of bizarre and eccentric behavior, it was no surprise when her legal team relied on an insanity defense at trial. Unfortunately for LaBarre, the jury rejected that plea and found her both sane and guilty. In June 2008, she was sentenced to life in prison with no possibility of parole.

Sheila LaBarre is currently serving her sentence at Homestead Correctional Institution in Florida City, Florida. The true number of her victims remains unknown. Most experts agree that it is probably more than the two she confessed to.

Miyoko Sumida

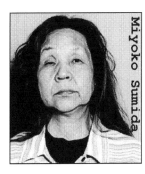

Japan is a law-abiding country, with a crime rate that ranks among the lowest in the world. Over 126 million souls inhabit its four main islands and yet the nation experiences less than 1,000 homicides per year. Tokyo is ranked as the safest city on the planet. Osaka is third on the list. Several other Japanese cities make the top twenty.

And yet, despite these enviable numbers, the nation of Japan has produced some truly horrific killers in its recent history, individuals like the cannibalistic pedophile Tsutomu Miyazaki, torture slayers Futoshi Matsunaga and Junko Ogata, and the Aum Shinrikyo cult, responsible for the 1995 saran gas attack on the Tokyo subway system. Another name that can now be added to this lexicon of evil is a notorious murder-for-profit killer named Miyoko Sumida.

On the face of it, Sumida made a very unlikely serial killer. She was a 64-year-old grandmother, living in the gritty industrial city of Amagasaki, near Osaka on the east coast of Japan's main island, Honshu. But delve a little deeper and there were things about Sumida that looked decidedly suspicious. For one thing, there was her unexplained wealth. With no visible means of support, she lived in a luxurious condominium, fitted out with the most opulent furnishings. She particularly loved jewelry and would often show off her favorite pieces to friends and neighbors, boasting that her entire collection was worth over $2 million. And how was this high school dropout, this former tavern owner, this barely literate pensioner able to afford such luxuries? How had she made her fortune? She'd done it through murder.

Miyoko Sumida was born in Hyōgo Prefecture, Japan in 1948. We know little about her early life except that she was a high school dropout who opened a bar in the entertainment district of Amagasaki when she was still a teenager. That was a daunting undertaking for someone so young, but Sumida appears to have been both shrewd and determined and she made it work. At 23, she married for the first time, but it didn't last, ending in divorce within two years. She later wed a man named Hisayoshi Sumida with whom she would have a son, Yutaro. This was a far happier union which endured until 2005, when disaster struck.

The Sumidas had been vacationing with friends in Okinawa and had taken a day trip to Cape Manzamo, one of the island's most popular tourist attractions. There they were posing for photographs with nine other people when Hisayoshi slipped and fell, plunging to his death on the rocks below. As a result of that accident, Miyoko received an insurance payout of 90 million yen (around $800,000) from her husband's life policy. The mortgage on her house was also settled in full. Perhaps that is what inspired her taste for easy money and the high life.

We can't know for sure when Miyoko Sumida started her killing spree, but we do know that at least six people connected to her disappeared between the years 2005 and 2011. Usually Sumida had a financial interest in their deaths, via a bequest or an insurance policy. Others who mysteriously vanished were owed considerable sums of money by her. These loans and bequests allowed her to substantially upgrade her lifestyle. In 2008, she purchased one of the largest units in an upscale condominium complex.

The condo included a vast veranda with a storage shed, masked from outside view by a wooden fence. Soon Sumida would be putting this feature to good use. In the meantime, she decorated lavishly and splurged on jewelry. She also started assembling a close-knit unit around her, including her sister-in-law, Mieko, her cousin Masanori, her son Yutaro, and Yutaro's wife, Rui. All of these individuals took up residence at the condo, where Miyoko ruled over them like a feudal warlord. The Japanese media would later dub this collective the 'Piranha Family.'

But that lay in the future. For now, Sumida and her cohorts were living the high life, funded by blood money. The first to die by their hands was 53-year-old Jiro Hashimoto. Hashimoto was a distant relative of Miyoko Sumida and had been living at her condo. But sometime in 2008, she instructed her gang to turn on him, to beat him into submission and then to lock him in the storage shed she kept on the balcony. There he would remain for over a week without food, while the gang frequently beat and tortured him. Their purpose was to extort money from his family and they managed to extract 64 million yen before their victim expired from starvation and from his injuries.

The murder of Jiro Hashimoto would form the template for at least four other killings. Also starved and beaten to death were Sumida's 66-year-old neighbor Kazuko Oe; 29-year-old Mariko Nakashima, the sister of Piranha family member Rui Sumida; Takashi Tanimoto, Sumida's 68-year-old uncle; and 71-year-old Mitsue Ando, who had been the long-term partner of Miyoko Sumida's deceased elder brother. And these were by no means the only victims. Four others – including Jiro Hashimoto's mother – remain missing.

In addition to their horrific murder method, the Piranhas also developed a macabre system of body disposal. Their preferred strategy was to cram the corpses into steel drums which they would then fill with concrete and dump in the ocean. It was certainly efficient, but it was also a rather unique signature, and it would lead, ultimately, to the gang's downfall.

In November 2011, police in Hyogo Prefecture received a tip-off that led them to an empty warehouse in Amagasaki. There, they found a 55-gallon steel drum which turned out to contain the remains of an elderly woman, later identified as Kazuko Oe, missing since September. An autopsy would reveal that the victim had been beaten and starved prior to her death. The police also learned that Oe had recently made a substantial loan to her neighbor, Miyoko Sumida, and that immediately made Sumida a suspect. Those suspicions only deepened when officers discovered three more bodies in October 2012. These were wrapped in blankets and hidden under the floorboards of an abandoned house. Checking the title deeds of the property, detectives found a familiar name. The house belonged to Miyoko Sumida. The victims were Mitsue Ando, Mariko Nakashima, and Takashi Tanimoto, all connected to Sumida and her family in some way.

Three weeks later, on October 30, a steel drum bobbed to the surface of the harbor in Bizen, about 80 miles south of Amagasaki. It was found to contain the brutalized remains of 53-year-old Jiro Hashimoto, another Sumida associate. It was then that the police started preparing the warrants for Sumida and the other Piranha family members. On December 11, 2012, officers moved in and took the entire gang into custody.

Whether out of fear or out of loyalty to Sumida, the gang members had very little to say to the police under interrogation. But Sumida was far more forthcoming. She spoke readily to detectives, admitting to the murders but insisting that she, and she alone, was responsible. There was, however, one death that Sumida would not discuss – that of her husband. Investigators had since received information that Hisayoshi Sumida's death might not have been an accident after all. A family friend told them that Miyoko had been encouraging her husband to take his own life for some time. She had been pressing him on the issue on the very morning that he flung himself from the clifftop. Investigators now believed that he had done so at his wife's urging. If that was true, it was one of the strangest murders that the Japanese police had ever encountered.

Miyoko, however, was mum about her husband's death, preferring to talk about her own. "I want to die," she told one of her jailers. "How can I kill myself?" That remark prompted prison officials to place her on a round-the-clock suicide watch, with a guard sent to check on her every fifteen minutes.

But if there is one thing that we have learned about Miyoko Sumida, it is that she was an extraordinarily determined woman. On December 12, 2012, one day after her arrest, Sumida was found lying unresponsive on the cot in her cell. She had been fine on the guard's previous pass. Sumida was rushed to the prison hospital, but it was already too late. Somehow she had managed to tear a strip of cloth from a sheet and to choke herself to death with it.

Michelle Michael

Growing up in Clarksburg, West Virginia, Michelle Goots was a golden girl, an overachiever who excelled academically, did well at sports, and shone as a cheerleader. The pretty, dark-haired Shelley was also popular, her peppy, upbeat personality gaining her a large circle of friends. After graduating high school, she stayed close to home and attended the University of West Virginia, where she continued to be a high-flyer. But just a year into college came the first bump of her thus far smooth ride. She fell pregnant.

The relationship between Michelle and her baby's father did not endure, not even until the birth. Nonetheless, the young, unwed mother was determined to provide for her son and thus returned to college as soon as she was able. By now, she had decided to pursue a nursing degree. She also reignited an old passion and joined the cheerleading squad. Soon after, she met a man named Robert Angus who she would later marry. By the time she graduated in 1997, she had a second child, a daughter.

Shelley Angus's first nursing job was at West Virginia University's Ruby Memorial Hospital in Morgantown, WV. There she was assigned to the pediatric unit and soon struck up a friendship with a co-worker, respiratory therapist Jimmy Michael. Like Shelley, Jimmy was married with two children and, like her, his marriage was in trouble. The two often consoled one another over their respective problems. Over time, their relationship deepened and became an affair. In late 1999, they decided they wanted to be together and both filed for divorce. They were married in May of 2000, just three months after Jimmy's divorce was finalized.

Jimmy's parents were thrilled at the union. His new bride was fun, outgoing, educated, and an excellent mom to both her kids and Jimmy's. The couple soon purchased a home, just a few minutes' drive from Ruby Memorial. Jimmy became the coach of their sons' football team while Shelley helped out with their daughters' cheerleading. They seemed like the perfect family.

And things were moving ahead on the career front, too. Shelley had resumed her studies part-time, eventually obtaining her Master's and qualifying as a Nurse Practitioner. Jimmy, meanwhile, had started his own business, providing medical equipment to housebound patients. That was in 2002. Three years later, Shelley decided that she was also ready for a career change. Through the kids' sporting activities, she and Jimmy had befriended another couple, Bobby and Kelly Teets, who were starting a business manufacturing bespoke sports and cheerleading uniforms for school teams. When they offered Shelley the chance to come on board, she jumped at it. She loved nursing but hated shift work.

On November 17, 2005, Shelley took a trip to Chicago with Bobby Teets to attend a conference on the embroidery industry. This was important to the business they were planning, and Shelley firmly committed to her new path by placing an order for an embroidery machine at the event. She returned home flushed with excitement about her new career path. For now, though, she continued working at the hospital.

The morning of November 29, 2005, was an ordinary one in the Michael household. Shelley was working an early shift that day and rose at 6 a.m., being careful not to wake her husband. She was out of the door at 6:30 and pulling into the parking lot at Ruby Memorial some five minutes later. But what had started out as a typical day would be rudely interrupted at 10:45, when Shelley received an urgent phone call from one of her neighbors. Her house was on fire.

Shelley rushed home immediately, arriving as firefighters were just getting the fierce blaze under control. A series of frantic phone calls established that her children were all safely at school. However, she couldn't reach Jimmy, and the reason would soon become tragically clear. When firemen entered the gutted home, they discovered a body, burned beyond recognition, in the master bedroom. Told about this, Shelley seemed surprisingly calm. "Are you sure?" was her only response.

Of course, the police could not be sure. The body was so badly burned that visual identification was impossible. It would take comparison with dental charts later that day to confirm what everyone already suspected. The victim was Jimmy Michael. The autopsy would also reveal one more stunning truth. Jimmy had not been killed by the blaze. The absence of smoke in his lungs indicated that he had already been dead when the fire started. This was now a homicide inquiry.

Morgantown Fire Chief Ken Tennant was the man tasked with determining the cause of the fire. In an investigation of this nature, one of the first tasks is to determine whether an accelerant had been used. Almost always, the answer is yes, but not in this case. However, one unusual feature of the blaze interested Tennant. In the bedroom where Jimmy Michael had died, the fire had reached a fierce intensity in one particular spot, burning through the floor and through the ceiling of the room below. This peculiar burn pattern would prove crucial in unraveling a mystery surrounding the case.

That revelation, however, was yet to come. For now, the police were working two angles, trying to determine Jimmy's cause of death and checking on the alibis of those close to him. The first question was resolved when the dead man's organs were examined and turned up massive amounts of the drug rocuronium. This is commonly used in surgery, to stop a patient's natural breathing when he is placed on a breathing apparatus. If, however, the apparatus is not started immediately, the patient will be unable to breathe and will suffocate within minutes. This was what had happened to Jimmy Michael. He would have been conscious throughout, slowly asphyxiating but unable to do anything about it.

But who would have murdered Jimmy in such a horrific way? The obvious suspect was his wife. As a pediatric intensive care nurse, she had access to rocuronium and knew how to administer it. She also had motive. Jimmy's life was insured for $500,000. The thing was that Shelley Michael had been at work when the fire started and had been seen by several of her co-workers. Her alibi looked unbreakable. But was it?

Looking through security footage, detectives soon spotted Shelley leaving the hospital at around 8 o'clock on the morning of the murder. The cameras next picked her up in the parking lot, getting into her car and driving off. Seventeen minutes later, she's back and is seen walking across the hospital foyer. Where had she been during those seventeen minutes? Investigators questioned her neighbors and found one who had seen Shelley's car parked in her drive during that time frame. It was time for the police to bring Shelley in for questioning.

Shelley, of course, was unaware that the police had her on tape. She was asked if she had left the hospital at any time on the morning that her husband died, and she said no. She was then shown the video and immediately changed her story, saying that she had gone down to her car to fetch her pager. "Did you drive anywhere?" a detective asked. "No," was Shelley's emphatic response. Again the incriminating video was produced. Then Shelley suddenly remembered that it had been raining hard that day and that she had moved her car under cover. She denied, when asked, that she had left the hospital premises. An officer then told her that a witness had seen her car parked in the drive of her house just after 8 a.m.

"Okay, I was there," Shelley conceded. "But I didn't go inside." Her latest story was that she had gone home to get an invoice for her embroidery business, which was due that day. However, as she pulled into the drive, she realized that the document was right there beside her on the passenger seat. She'd then turned around and driven back to the hospital. Asked why she had lied about such a trivial thing, she said that she felt guilty for not going into the house and checking on Jimmy. "I might have saved him," she sniveled. After nearly eight hours on interrogation, she was allowed to leave.

Shelley's false and evasive statements convinced some on the investigative team that she was the person responsible for her husband's death. But others were skeptical, their doubts based primarily on the timeline. She had been spotted at the house just after eight, but firefighters had only been called at 10:15, when a neighbor spotted flames issuing from an upstairs window. If Shelley had started the fire, how was it possible that it had burned for two hours before anyone noticed?

The answer lay in that unusual burn pattern and the hole that had burned through to the room below. Investigators believed that Shelley had injected Jimmy with rocuronium before going to work. She had then started her shift in order to establish an alibi but had returned home at eight o'clock, once her children had left for school. Her plan was to start a fire that would destroy evidence, but the tight timescale meant that she could not hang around to ensure that the blaze had taken hold. She'd simply lit the bedding on fire and then fled, closing the bedroom door behind her.

But closing the door was a mistake. Fire needs oxygen to flourish and is extinguished when this vital fuel is absent. In this case, the burning bedclothes quickly sucked all of the air out of the sealed room and then receded to a glowing patch of carpet at the foot of the bed. Those embers had slowly smoldered over the next two hours, feeding on the small supply of oxygen coming through the floor boards. Eventually, it had burned through the boards and through the ceiling of the room below. The air then flowed through this gap serving as an accelerant, sparking the flame. Even a professional arsonist could not have set a more effective timing mechanism.

The mystery of the delayed conflagration had been explained. In addition, the police learned of another motive for murder. Shelley's visit to Chicago, a couple of weeks prior to the murder, had been more than just a business trip. Bobby Teets admitted that they had slept together during that trip and had continued their affair after returning to West Virginia. It appeared that Shelley had been ready to move on, with a new career and a new man. Her husband's $500,000 insurance policy would have provided a nice boost to the fresh start she had planned.

Shelley Michael was arrested and charged with murder on March 10, 2006. At trial, her defense continued to argue that the timeline ruled her out as a suspect. But the evidence to the contrary was powerful. In preparing for trial, Morgantown PD had called on the ATF for help in backing up the fire evidence. The federal agency had then conducted an experiment, building six full scale models of the Michael's master bedroom and running various scenarios. The "delayed blaze" theory turned out to be entirely feasible.

Found guilty of first-degree murder and guilty of arson, Michelle Michael was sentenced to life in prison. The jury did, however, make a recommendation of mercy, meaning that Michael would be eligible for parole in 15 years. On the charge of arson, the judge added a 20-year term with parole eligibility in five. Since the terms run consecutively, Shelley Michael will serve at least two decades behind bars.

Lastania Abarta

She was 18 years old and a renowned beauty from a middle-class background; he was 40, born into one of Southern California's wealthiest Hispanic families, and a notorious womanizer. It was by no means certain that the lives of Lastania Abarta and Francisco "Chico" Forster would intersect, but intersect they did, with explosive results. The story of their brief relationship would become one of the most sensational in 1880s Los Angeles.

The first time that Chico set eyes on Lastania was at a billiards parlor owned by her father. Chico had been shooting a few frames when he was distracted by a beautiful voice – Lastania, playing the guitar and singing, as she often did to entertain her father's clientele. Captivated, Chico went over and introduced himself. It did not go as he might have hoped. Lastania was polite but standoffish, quite unlike the women Chico typically targeted. Usually his winning smile and well-worked line of flattery had them swooning and ready to do his bidding. But not Lastania. She was a virtuous girl raised in a strict Catholic family. She was also engaged to be married. That only made Chico more determined to have his way with her.

Over the weeks that followed, Chico became a regular at the billiards parlor although his interest now was less on the games and more on the beautiful chanteuse. Over time, Lastania warmed to him. She even agreed to meet with him outside the parlor although she always insisted that her older sister Hortensia accompany them as chaperone. To Chico, this was progress, and he started pestering Lastania to break off her engagement and marry him instead. "Why would you marry that black Indian?" he mocked, referring to Lastania's fiancé who was, in fact, a prominent lawyer of excellent reputation.

And perhaps those jibes began to get to Lastania because she started to seriously consider Chico's marriage proposal, unorthodox though it was. When he showed her a marriage license and asked her to elope with him to Phoenix, Arizona, she was ready to listen. In March 1881, after Lastania performed at a party given by California governor Pio Pico, the couple made their break, booking in at the Moiso Mansion Hotel for the night, with plans to travel to Arizona the next morning.

What Lastania didn't realize was that it was all a hoax. The marriage certificate that Chico had shown her was a forgery. He had no plans to leave L.A., no plans to wed. The whole thing was a ruse to get Lastania into a hotel room, where Chico hoped to seduce her. Unfortunately for him, the bride-to-be was not prepared to surrender her virginity until the nuptials were concluded. Chico slept that night on the couch.

Over the next three days, Lastania remained sequestered at the hotel while Chico went about his business, supposedly finalizing their travel plans and arranging for a priest to marry them in Arizona. Every evening he returned, to tell her that progress was being made and that they'd soon be on their way. He'd then try to pressure her into sleeping with him, becoming increasingly forceful when she refused.

Finally, on the third day, Chico played his ace. He told Lastania that her reputation was already ruined since everyone knew that she'd spent three days and nights in a hotel room with him. She might as well surrender herself, he said. Then they could be married and she'd regain her status as a respectable woman. Should she refuse, he'd walk away, although he'd make it known that they had enjoyed conjugal relations. Who'd want to marry her then? She'd be spoiled goods. Faced with this horrible dilemma, Lastania eventually gave in. Chico took her virginity that night and she cried herself to sleep. When she woke in the morning, he was gone.

And thus began the second chapter of this sordid tale. Now that he'd finally bedded Lastania, Chico lost all interest in her and went on to pursue other conquests. When she tracked him down and pressed him on the issue of marriage, he told her that he would fulfill his obligation as soon as he was able to find a priest who was prepared to marry them. Thus far, his search had been in vain.

While all of this was going on, a whispering campaign had begun. Lastania's reputation was in ruins and her fiancé had called off the engagement. Even her own mother had disowned her. Her only hope of redemption was for Chico to fulfill his promise, something he appeared disinclined to do. Desperate, the young woman decided to take her own life and bought a revolver for that purpose. She might have gone through with it, too, had Hortensia not arrived in the nick of time to stop her.

In fact, Hortensia remained Lastania's only ally, taking up the fight on behalf of her sister and pressuring Chico to do the right thing. On March 16, 1881, the sisters tracked him down to a horse racing track, where Hortensia berated him for his ungentlemanly conduct. Chico then offered up his usual excuse, saying that he would marry Lastania as soon as he could find a priest willing to perform the ceremony. This time, however, Hortensia called his bluff. She said that she had already made the arrangements and insisted that Chico accompany them to the church right away. Eager to avoid a scene, he complied.

In a modern context, it might be difficult to understand why Lastania was so determined to marry Chico. The man was quite obviously a cad, who used and abused women and then discarded them when he'd had his way. A marriage to him would not have been a happy one. But all of that was secondary when compared to the shame that Lastania would have to endure as a "fallen woman." She had surrendered her virginity to a man who was not her husband. That carried a stigma that she would not live down. Her only hope was marriage.

But Lastania should have known that Chico was not the marrying kind. As soon as they were clear of the racetrack, he ordered the cab driver to stop, and then got out and started walking away. The sisters then alighted the carriage themselves and gave chase, with Hortensia calling after Chico and Lastania following at a distance. Then Chico stopped to engage with Hortensia, and it was at this point that Lastania took decisive action. The jilted bride drew her revolver, walked up to Chico and fired a single bullet, hitting him in the right eye and killing him where he stood. As he collapsed to the ground, a bystander approached and disarmed Lastania. She was held until the police arrived and placed her under arrest, charging her with premeditated murder.

From the moment that news of the sensational shooting hit the headlines, there was an outpouring of public support for Lastania. Chico was depicted in the media as a rogue and a scoundrel, who had seduced an innocent young girl and deflowered her under false pretenses. Effectively, it was rape, and Lastania (at least in public opinion) had been entitled to avenge herself, to take steps to restore her honor. But public opinion held little sway with lawmakers. The Forster family was rich, famous, and demanding justice. Chico's father even hired a special prosecutor to try the case. He was determined to see Lastania swing from the gallows for her crime.

As the matter came before the courts, Lastania's lawyer caused a stir by entering a not guilty plea on her behalf, stating that he intended to prove that his client was suffering from temporary insanity at the time of the shooting. No less than seven medical experts were trotted out to support this hypothesis, stating that Lastania had displayed classic symptoms of "female hysteria" when she pulled the trigger on Chico Forster. The most emphatic of these was Dr. Joseph Kurtz who told the court that, "Any virtuous woman, when deprived of her virtue, would go mad, undoubtedly." That earned him a standing ovation from the public gallery. It also earned Lastania Abarta an acquittal, with the all-male jury taking just 20 minutes to reach its decision.

We know very little of Lastania's life after the conclusion of her sensational murder trial. Supposedly, she left California, never to return. And despite her fears of being "ruined," it is believed that she later married and remained so until the end of her life.

Shirley Withers

Shirley Withers was hardly the kind of woman to turn heads. Dowdy and heavyset, with an unflattering hairstyle, the 33-year-old bookkeeper probably expected to be left on the shelf. So when a stranger struck up a conversation with her at a party in 2000, Shirley was more than receptive. Only later would she find out that her mystery suitor was a multi-millionaire property developer and luxury car dealer.

Peter Shellard could probably have dated a supermodel had he so desired. But then Shellard had never been a man to do things by the book. Eccentric was a word often used to describe him. In the upmarket Melbourne, Australia suburb where he lived, he infuriated neighbors by torching the historic garden of his late nineteenth-century mansion and replacing it with chicken runs and shipping containers for his car business. By night, he could be found cruising the streets in his open top Rolls Royce, usually headed for one of the city's S & M clubs. He was prone to mood swings and had been diagnosed as bipolar. And now he added another eccentricity. He decided that frumpy, overweight Shirley Withers was the love of his life.

Shellard's pursuit of Withers was typically over the top. He showered his new girlfriend with gifts, a new car, even a house. When she expressed an interest in starting a fashion business, he set her up with a boutique in upscale Brighton. He also made her his personal bookkeeper, with access to his company accounts. Shirley Withers must have thought that she'd landed in a fairy tale and was playing the role of Cinderella.

But that rosy picture would have been a misinterpretation of what was really going on. The problems started with the boutique. Withers was no businesswoman and she was certainly no fashionista. The business was soon in trouble and bleeding cash, with suppliers cutting her off over unpaid bills. Seeking to rectify the situation, Shirley started dipping into Peter's other companies, forging his signature on checks to keep her boutique afloat. When she saw just how easy that was, she allowed greed to get the better of her and started writing checks for her personal use. It all escalated from there. But it did not go unnoticed.

Peter Shellard was a self-made man. He had not clawed his way to the top by being a fool. As soon as he noticed something awry, he called in his accountant and ordered an audit. That revealed the true extent of the fraud – as much as $900,000 was missing, and it was obvious who had taken it. That left Peter with two options. Either he could deal with this privately or he could take it to the police. Furious that the woman he'd trusted, to whom he'd been so generous, who he loved, had betrayed him, Shellard decided on the latter. First, though, he was going to confront Shirley.

The response, however, was not what Shellard had expected. Shirley flatly denied that she had taken the money, leaving him in a quandary. Despite her betrayal, he still loved her. He badly wanted to believe her story, even in the face of strong evidence to the contrary. The man who had made his fortune by being decisive and forceful was wavering.

And while he pondered his next move, Shirley was making hers. A police investigation was worrisome, but she did not believe that Peter would actually report the fraud. That would mean losing face and might cost him investors in future real estate projects. What really frightened her was being cut off from her affluent lifestyle. She was not about to give that up.

Enter into the picture a pair of low-life junkies named Stanley Callinicos and Sophia Stoupas. Shirley deliberately sought them out, befriended them, started financing their habit. In no time at all, she had them as trained as Pavlov's dogs, salivating on command, willing to do just about anything to hold onto their meal ticket. That was when she started spilling stories about her abusive boyfriend, who was into S&M and forced her to perform sexual acts that she found disgusting. She wanted badly to leave him, but she knew that he would never let her. The only way out was to kill him. Would they help? Of course they would.

On the night of Friday, May 6, 2005, Shirley Withers used her key to enter Peter Shellard's home. She ushered in her newfound friends. The trio then made their way to the master bedroom, where they found Shellard asleep. Rudely shaken awake, Shellard found himself confronted by three figures in the darkness. A brief struggle ensued, during which Shellard bit Sophia Stoupas's finger, drawing blood. However, he was easily overcome, struck on the head with a lamp and then handcuffed, his feet tied with a rope, and a pillow case pulled over his head. Then Shirley Withers took a syringe filled with heroin from her handbag and injected the drug into her lover and benefactor. Her intent was to cause an overdose, but Shirley wasn't taking any chances. She also inserted an OxyContin suppository in his rectum. This is an extremely powerful painkiller with serious side effects if given to the wrong person. Particularly at risk are those with heart problems. Withers was well aware that her boyfriend fell into that category. It was only a matter of time before the cocktail of drugs killed him.

In the early morning hours of May 7, a frantic 000 call was made to emergency services in Melbourne. An apparently distraught Shirley Withers was on the line, claiming that she had arrived at her boyfriend's house and found him dead. Police officers were soon on the scene and found 51-year-old Peter Shellard hogtied on the floor of the master bedroom, with a bloody pillowcase pulled over his head. Later, under questioning, Withers admitted that Peter had been into S & M and suggested that his death might have been the result of a sex game gone wrong. The police had their doubts about that theory, especially when the autopsy revealed defensive bruises. Shellard had put up a fight for his life. There was also the issue of drugs found in his system. Everyone who knew the abrasive businessman swore that he hated drugs and never used them.

Shirley Withers was, of course, a suspect in the murder. But if she had done it, what had been her motive? Shellard had left his entire fortune to his children, so Withers would not benefit financially from his death. In fact, she was now cast adrift from the lavish lifestyle she had become accustomed to during their five years together. His death had left her far worse off. Had she perhaps killed him in a fit of rage, perhaps during a lover's quarrel? Possible, but the scene suggested otherwise. This did not look like a spontaneous killing. It looked premeditated. That seemed to rule Shirley Withers out.

But then Withers put herself right back in the frame. With the house still taped off as a crime scene, she arrived and demanded access. Her purpose, she said, was to search for Peter Shellard's updated Will. Before his death, she claimed, Shellard had signed a new document, making her his sole heir. Whether or not this Will actually existed, Withers clearly believed that it did. She'd had motive after all.

Things fell into place pretty quickly after that. Detectives learned of the money that had been stolen from Shellard's business; they heard from his ex-wife that he had feared for his life; they found a cigarette butt at the scene when Shellard was a non-smoker who strictly forbade smoking in his house. Then came the first forensic breakthrough, a bloody smear found on a telephone. It turned out to be the fingerprint of someone with a police record. Sophia Stoupas was well-known as a drug addict and petty criminal. She was also known to keep company with another junkie, Stanley Callinicos.

But how might these two deadbeats be linked to Shirley Withers? The circles they moved in were worlds apart. In order to find out the answer to that question, investigators obtained permission to run a tap on Withers's phone. Soon, they had a startling admission on tape. During a conversation with a friend, Withers said that she knew who had killed Peter. It was a couple of "druggies" and she was planning to get back at them for what they'd done. "I'll kill them with my own hands and make the bastards suffer," she said.

How genuine was this threat? The police took it very seriously indeed. They believed that Withers was planning to murder her accomplices in order to cover her tracks. And so they sent in an undercover cop posing as a hit-man and offering to do the job for a fee. Withers was more than happy to meet his price. Not only that, but she provided the officer with a full background, describing the murder of Peter Shellard in great detail, all of it captured on tape.

Shirley Withers, Stanley Callinicos, and Sophia Stoupas were arrested soon after, with the latter two pleading guilty to manslaughter and accepting six-year sentences. Withers, meanwhile, decided to take her chances with the courts. She pleaded not guilty at her 2007 trial, but the jury didn't believe her. She was convicted on one count of murder and two counts of incitement to murder. The sentence was 26 years, but a sympathetic judge would downgrade her conviction to manslaughter on appeal and cut her jail time in half. He was apparently convinced by Withers's story that she had never intended to kill Peter but had only wanted to "teach him a lesson."

LaFonda Foster and Tina Powell

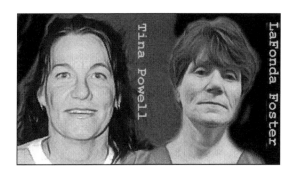

LaFonda Foster and Tina Powell were bad news. The pair were drunks and drug addicts, ex-cons, occasional prostitutes, hostile individuals always spoiling for a fight. It is a wonder that anyone would have chosen to hang out with them but, amazingly, they were part of a loosely affiliated clique of drinkers and addicts, a group that included 45-year-old Virginia Kearns and her partially disabled husband, Carlos, aged 73.

On the afternoon of April 23, 1986, police in Lexington, Kentucky, received a call from Virginia Kearns, complaining that there were two drunk and aggressive women in her apartment who were refusing to leave. Officers responded to the address at around 4 p.m. and found the two individuals Kearns had complained about. But LaFonda Foster and Tina Powell weren't intoxicated and they weren't acting aggressively. Instead, it was Kearns who was obviously drunk and quite belligerent. After warning her against making false reports, the officers left.

Later that evening, a spontaneous party broke out in a parking lot adjacent to the Kearns's apartment building. Powell and Foster were quick to join in the festivities, but they arrived empty-handed and resorted to scrounging drinks and cigarettes from their fellow revelers. Powell also tried to sell a hunting knife to several partygoers, but there were no takers. Then the pair spotted Virginia Kearns heading out and followed her to a nearby drug store. There, a shopper saw them pushing and shaking Kearns and demanding money. Kearns said that she didn't have any on her and suggested that they come with her back to her apartment where her husband, Carlos, would help them out.

But Carlos didn't have any cash either, and now Foster and Powell were starting to get angry. In fact, they became so threatening that Carlos Kearns eventually agreed to write them a check for $25. That seemed to mollify the women, but they now demanded the Kearns's car keys so that they could drive to the local Quik Cash. They also insisted that Virginia and Carlos, along with Carlos's live-in caregiver, Trudy Harrell, accompany them. With no option but to comply, the Kearnses agreed. They were just about to leave when Roger Keene and Theodore Sweet, friends of the theirs, arrived at the apartment. They too were coerced into going along for the ride.

With Foster behind the wheel, Powell in the passenger seat, and five adults crammed into the back, the unlikely band set off. The check was cashed sometime between 6 and 7 p.m., but still Foster and Powell were dissatisfied. They wanted to buy cocaine and $25 wasn't going to cut it. They therefore drove to the home of another associate, Lester Luttrell, and tried to intimidate some cash out of him. But Luttrell wasn't in a giving mood that night, and he turned them away. Before departing, Foster drew a .22 and fired a round through the window of Luttrell's home.

What is truly remarkable about this whole episode is that none of the hostages made any attempt to escape. Even when Foster and Powell left them unattended in the vehicle, the five of them made no effort to flee. There may be a few reasons for this. Firstly, the disabled Carlos Kearns couldn't run, and his wife, and possibly Trudy Harrell, wouldn't leave him. Keene and Sweet might have remained out of loyalty to their friends. Perhaps they thought there was strength in numbers. More likely, they were afraid to cross LaFonda Foster, who had a fearsome reputation. Either way, their indecision would prove costly.

At around 8:25 p.m. that evening, a car pulled to a stop at a field off Mount Tabor Road. LaFonda Foster and Tina Powell exited the vehicle, then forced their terrified hostages out and ordered them to lie face down on the grass. Foster then told Powell to "cut them," which she did, working her way up and down the line, slashing and stabbing while Foster held a gun on the victims. Then Foster started firing, pumping bullets into the prone figures. Miraculously, although shot at close range, none of the victims was killed. This was because Foster's weapon was a barely functional .22, a "Saturday Night Special" bought on the street for just $10. It was also loaded with old ammunition.

But perhaps it would have been better for the victims had they been killed. Now they were rounded up again and forced back into the car, all except Trudy Harrell. On the way out of the field, Foster deliberately drove over Harrell, dragging her under the vehicle for 225 feet before coming to a stop in the Berke Plaza parking lot. There the body was dragged out, shot in the head and stabbed several times for

good measure. Trudy Harrell was the first to die that night. She would
not be the last.

Foster and Powell's tally of hostages had been reduced from five to
four. But now the killers had a problem. Foster's gun was out of
bullets. Stopping at a nearby tavern, Powell managed to cadge a few
.22 rounds from a bartender she knew. She told him that she needed
the ammunition to "shoot some rats."

A short while later, one of those bullets would end the life of Virginia
Kearns. Virginia was pulled from the car and shot to death behind a
paint shop, while her husband looked on helplessly. The killers then
drove to another field, this one off Richmond and Squires Roads.
There, a similar fate would befall Roger Keene, shot twice in the back
of the head and once in the ear. Theodore Sweet was shot, too, but
Foster had grown impatient, and so she finished the job by driving
over the injured man. That left just Carlos Kearns alive, and his would
be the most dreadful fate of all. The disabled 73-year-old was locked
in the car. The vehicle was then doused with gasoline and set alight.
Kearns was burned alive.

By now, the Lexington Police Department was dealing with one of the
most violent nights in its history. Calls kept coming in, reporting the
discovery of horribly mutilated bodies. The cops had no idea, at this
point, that the murders had been committed by the same two
perpetrators and that those perps were women. That would only come
to light when they received a report from Humana Hospital on
Richmond Road. Two women had entered the building covered in
blood. Assuming they were injured, staff had rushed to their
assistance. The women, however, had waved them away, saying that

they just needed to wash up. They'd then gone into a restroom.
LaFonda Foster and Tina Powell were arrested in the hospital parking
lot, while they stood waiting for a taxi.

Foster and Powell were taken to a nearby police station, where they
were questioned separately. Their explanations for their bloody
clothing was remarkably similar. They claimed that they had gotten
into a fight with each other but that their differences had now been
resolved. But that story was never going to fly, not with that much
blood and no obvious injuries to either of the women. Still, the police
hadn't yet made the connection between these two blood-spattered
individuals and the spate of homicides that had been reported that
night. Foster and Powell were arrested only for public intoxication.
They were taken to the Fayette County Detention Center, where they
were allowed to clean up. During that process, Foster tried to dispose
of evidence by flushing her bloody socks and shoestrings down the
toilet.

But that would prove to be a vain effort. Detectives were starting to
piece the puzzle together. A bloody knife had been found in Powell's
possession, while Foster had been carrying three .22 caliber bullets in
her pocket. Eyewitness reports were starting to come in – from the
Quik Cash clerk; from the bartender; from the drug store shopper;
from the parking lot revelers. The police had a description of the
suspects, and it closely matched Foster and Powell. Then they found
the burned-out car, with Foster's .22 discarded nearby. In no time at
all, Foster and Powell found themselves charged with something way
more serious than public drunkenness. They were arraigned on five
counts of first-degree murder.

This wasn't a difficult case to solve, and it wasn't a difficult case to prove in a court of law. The only question was the potential fate of the defendants, and the prosecutor was quick to clear that up. He would be seeking the death penalty against both women. That most likely scared Tina Powell into turning on her co-defendant. In court, Powell's counsel revealed that his client and LaFonda Foster were lovers and that Foster totally dominated her. Powell even used Battered Wife Syndrome as part of her defense. As tenuous as this seems, it achieved its aim. Powell avoided the death penalty and was sentenced to 25 years to life instead.

LaFonda Foster's lawyers also had a few tricks up their sleeves. They contended that their client had endured a lifetime of abuse and battery at the hands of men and that this had caused her to become emotionally disturbed, drug-addicted, and violent toward others. She was as much a victim, they claimed, as the people she'd killed.

But this was perhaps a defense that stretched incredulity too far. The jury rejected it and returned a verdict of guilty. LaFonda Foster was sentenced to death, although that sanction was later commuted on appeal. In 1991, she was re-sentenced to life in prison without parole. The killing spree that she and Tina Powell perpetrated remains the bloodiest in Kentucky's history.

Marjorie Ann Orbin

When 26-year-old Jay Orbin walked into a Las Vegas strip joint in the summer of 1985, he had no idea that he would end up falling in love. But one of the dancers, a lithe blonde named Marjorie, made a big impression on him, so much so that Jay waited around until she finished her gig and then introduced himself. Thereafter, he became a regular at the club and he and Marjorie became friends. Jay also pestered her to go out with him and, although she initially said no, he eventually wore her down. A couple of dates followed before Jay suggested that they make the relationship more permanent. Marjorie, just 24 at the time, wasn't ready for that. But she couldn't bring herself to tell Jay to his face and so she quit her job and moved back home to Florida without letting him know. Jay was left to nurse a broken heart.

For Marjorie, though, the move marked the beginning of a decade-long adventure. Back in the Sunshine State, she hooked up with Michael J. Peter, a multi-millionaire who owned and operated strip clubs around the world. Peter was also a budding filmmaker, and he contracted Marjorie to appear as a star dancer in his movie, "No More Dirty Deals." She was also the chief choreographer on the production. Soon the two of them were involved in a relationship and engaged to be married. Then followed a whirlwind of travel to exotic locations, all of it first-class.

Marjorie was living the life, but there was one thing that she found difficult to deal with. Her fiancé had a roving eye and, surrounded 24/7 by beautiful women, he had ample opportunity to sate his desires. Marjorie was a jealous woman by nature, and eventually Peter's dalliances started to wear on her. One day, she simply packed a bag and walked out on him. Thereafter, she drifted into a series of relationships and a number of failed marriages. By 1993, she was back in Vegas, working the strip clubs. Then, out of the blue, she got a call from an old friend she hadn't heard from in ten years.

Jay Orbin had been driving to Las Vegas from his home in Phoenix, Arizona, when he'd spotted Marjorie's picture on a billboard for a strip club. Jay was still unmarried, but the intervening years had been good to him. He had built a successful business selling Native American jewelry and art and spent much of his time on the road hawking his wares. That is what had brought him to Vegas and an unexpected reunion with Marjorie. After hooking up for a drink, the two of them spent the entire night talking. Before Jay left the next morning, he asked Marjorie to move to Phoenix to be with him.

Marjorie was by now in her mid-thirties, and she must have known that her career as a professional dancer was nearing its endgame. Jay was perhaps not her idea of the perfect man, but he was well off and shared many of the same ideals that she did. Most importantly, he wanted kids. Despite being told at age 18 that she'd never bear children, Marjorie longed to be a mother. Jay promised to pay for the best fertility doctors available if she would agree to be his wife, and perhaps that was what swung it. They married at the Little White Wedding Chapel on Las Vegas Boulevard in 1994.

Back in Phoenix, Jay Orbin's family was less than enamored with Marjorie, who they took to be a gold digger. But despite her glamorous exterior and her background as an exotic dancer, Marjorie proved to be a quite conventional housewife, one who appeared happy to clean and do laundry and cook her husband's meals. And then, in late 1995, came the joyous news. The fertility treatments had paid off. Marjorie was pregnant. A son, Noah, was born in August the following year.

For a time, it appeared that the Orbins were living the ideal life. Jay's business was doing well, and the money was rolling in; home life was idyllic, and both parents were besotted with their little boy; even Jay's family had come to accept Marjorie and even to like her.

And then, in the blink of an eye, it all came crashing down. August 26, 2004, was Noah Orbin's eighth birthday. Jay and Marjorie had hosted a party for him, attended by friends and family. The following day, Jay departed on an extended sales trip to Florida. He was to have been away for a few weeks, but the weather turned bad, with Hurricane Francis tearing through the state, bringing flooding and devastation. Jay was forced to cut his losses and head home early. The upside was that he'd arrive in Phoenix on September 8. He would get to spend his 45th birthday with his wife and son.

We know that Jay made it to Phoenix that day because he was just driving into town when his mother called to wish him happy birthday.

Jay told her that he was almost home and said that he'd phone her later that evening. It was a call that he would never make.

A week passed with no word from Jay and with his family growing increasingly concerned. The only one who appeared relaxed about his sudden disappearance was Marjorie. Asked about Jay's whereabouts, she said that he had arrived home on September 8, had spent the evening, and had then departed on another sales trip. That story had a ring of authenticity to it, since Jay was a hard-working man who was often on the road. But he always checked in at least once a day and now, Marjorie had to admit, he had not done so. Jay's family then prevailed on her to report him missing. Eventually, after much persuasion, she did.

The missing person case was assigned to Detective Jan Butcher of Phoenix PD. And it did not take long for Butcher to begin suspecting that Marjorie Orbin might be involved in her husband's disappearance. Marjorie's somewhat cavalier attitude was one thing, but she was also uncooperative with the investigation. When Butcher asked her for the license plate number of Jay's vehicle, she said that she did not know it and would have to call back. She failed to do so. It would take the detective three calls and several messages to get the information. And then there was the spending spree. In the days following Jay Orbin's mysterious vanishing, his wife withdrew $45,000 from his business bank account. Much of the money was splurged on luxury items, including a $12,000 baby grand piano. This only served to heighten Det. Butcher's suspicions. Eventually, she decided to ask Marjorie to submit to a polygraph. Then followed a strange telephone interlude between the two women.

Det. Butcher: "Can we schedule you for a polygraph?"

Marjorie (speaking to someone else in the room): "She wants me to take a polygraph tomorrow."

Male voice in the background: "Tell her to go f*ck herself."

The angry male voice heard by Butcher turned out to belong to a man named Larry Weisberg. As the detective started probing, she quickly learned that Weisberg worked out at the same gym as Marjorie and that the two of them had been having an affair. Weisberg, it appeared, had even moved into the Orbin residence since Jay's disappearance. He was also fiercely protective of Marjorie. When Butcher arrived at the house the next day to execute a search warrant, Weisberg tried to attack the SWAT team that had been brought along to support the detectives. That turned out to be a bad mistake. Weisberg was Tasered and his nose was smashed in the subsequent melee. He was also arrested.

But Marjorie had bigger problems to deal with than bailing out her boyfriend. The search had turned up several pieces on incriminating evidence, including Jay Orbin's credit cards and his business checkbook. If, as Marjorie claimed, Jay had left on another business trip, why had he not taken these essential items with him? It was at this point that Butcher was certain. Jay Orbin was not a missing person. He was a homicide victim.

On October 23, 2004, six weeks after Jay Orbin went missing, a
transient came across a plastic barrel, abandoned in the desert on the
outskirts of Phoenix. He decided to open it and got the shock of his
life. Crammed inside was the headless, armless torso of a man, devoid
of all internal organs and intestines. These were the only parts of Jay
Orbin's corpse that would ever be recovered.

With the case now transferred to the homicide division, it fell to
Detective David Barnes to pick up where Det. Butcher had left off.
One thing remained constant, however, the identity of the prime
suspect. Marjorie Orbin was brought in for another round of
questioning but denied having anything to do with her husband's
death. When she was eventually arrested, three weeks later, it was not
for murder but for fraud. She had tried to use Jay's credit card at a
Circuit City store.

Meanwhile, evidence in the homicide case continued to mount.
Investigators found receipts for mops and cleaning products purchased
one day after Jay went missing; they learned that Marjorie had had the
garage floor epoxy coated just the next day; they found surveillance
footage from a Lowe's store showing Marjorie buying two plastic
barrels exactly like the one Jay's remains had been found in. On
December 6, six weeks after her husband's dismembered body was
discovered, Marjorie Orbin was taken into custody and charged with
his murder.

It would be five long years before the matter eventually came to trial.
By then, Marjorie's defense team had come up with a new narrative.
They now admitted that their client had been involved in Jay's death
but only as an accessory. According to this version of events, Jay had

returned early from his trip to Florida and had caught Larry Weisberg
in his house. An altercation had ensued during which Weisberg had
shot Jay. He had then warned Marjorie against going to the police,
saying that he would kill her and her son. He also coerced her into
participating in the cleanup and getting rid of the body.

There are a number of problems with this story. First, it is almost
certain that Jay was shot in the garage, not inside the house. This
suggests that he was ambushed as he entered and was not killed in an
altercation. Second, Marjorie's behavior in the aftermath was not that
of a woman whose husband had been murdered and had now been
forced into silence by his killer. If she was so afraid of Weisberg, why
had she continued her relationship with him? Third, the location of
Jay's remains suggested that they were intended to be found. This
could only be true if Marjorie's plan was to inherit, something she
could not have done if Jay remained missing.

These were the questions raised at trial by prosecutor Treena Kay. Kay
offered an alternative theory of Jay's murder, suggesting that Marjorie
had lain in wait and shot him as he entered the garage. She had then
dismembered the body with a jigsaw, later removing the blood
evidence by acid washing the concrete floor and then having it
resurfaced. She had later discarded the remains in the desert, along
with the jigsaw and the murder weapon, neither of which has ever
been found.

Support for the prosecution's version came from Larry Weisberg
himself. Called as a witness, he claimed that he had played no part in
the murder at all, not even in the disposal. He admitted under cross-
examination that Marjorie had never told him outright that she had

killed Jay. However, he said that there were other indicators, in particular, Marjorie's increasingly desperate behavior as the murder inquiry progressed. At one point, she had suggested that they run away together. He had refused.

Deputy County Attorney Kay also put Marjorie's former cellmate, Sophia Johnson, in the witness box. She claimed that the accused had admitted to her that she had shot her husband with his own gun. She'd done it, according to Johnson, because she hated Jay and found him fat and ugly, with disgusting table manners. However, she would not divorce him because she wanted his money. The jailhouse snitch also told the court, under questioning, that she had not been offered any reduction of sentence in exchange for her testimony. She was speaking out of her own volition.

Only one person spoke on behalf of Marjorie, her former fiancé Michael Peter. He claimed that he had contacted Marjorie during her marriage and asked her to come back to him. Marjorie, however, had refused, saying that Jay was a good man and that she would not deprive him of his son.

At this point, the defense stunned the courtroom by closing its case. Most had expected Marjorie to take the stand. She, herself, was keen to do so, but her lawyers advised against it. They felt that there was a more than reasonable doubt in the case, especially regarding the involvement of Larry Weisberg. Surely, the jury could not find Marjorie guilty.

But that is exactly how the jurors found, taking just seven hours to reach their decision. Marjorie Orbin was guilty of murder. The only concession to the defense was that the death penalty called for by the prosecution was rejected. The recommendation was life in prison.

Marjorie Orbin is currently serving her time at the Arizona State Prison Complex in Perryville, Arizona. It is a long way from the opulent lifestyle that she had killed for. Marjorie continues to protest her innocence, saying that it was Larry Weisberg who murdered her husband.

For more True Crime books by Robert Keller please visit

http://bit.ly/kellerbooks

Printed in Great Britain
by Amazon

44667237R00085